Disability Discrimination Act 1995

Code of Practice

Rights of Access

Goods, Facilities, Services and Premises

London: The Stationery Office

Applications for reproduction should be made in writing to the Disability Rights Commission, 2nd Floor, Arndale House, Arndale Centre, Manchester, M4 3AQ.

The information contained in this publication is believed to be correct at the time of manufacture. Whilst care has been taken to ensure that the information is accurate, the publisher can accept no responsibility for any errors or omissions or for changes to the details given.

A CIP catalogue record for this book is available from the British Library.

A Library of Congress CIP catalogue record has been applied for.

First published 2002

ISBN   0 11 702860 6

The Commencement date is May 27, 2002

This revised Code of Practice deals with the duties placed by Part III of the Disability Discrimination Act 1995 on those providing goods, facilities or services to the public and those selling, letting or managing premises. The Act makes it unlawful for service providers, landlords and other persons to discriminate against disabled people in certain circumstances.

The duties on service providers are being introduced in three stages:

■ since 2 December 1996 it has been unlawful for service providers to treat disabled people less favourably for a reason related to their disability;

■ since 1 October 1999 service providers have had to make 'reasonable adjustments' for disabled people, such as providing extra help or making changes to the way they provide their services; and

■ from 1 October 2004 service providers may have to make other 'reasonable adjustments' in relation to the physical features of their premises to overcome physical barriers to access.

The duties on landlords and other persons in connection with the selling, letting and managing of premises were introduced on 2 December 1996. Since that date, it has been unlawful for them to treat disabled people less favourably for a reason related to their disability. There is no equivalent duty to make 'reasonable adjustments' in relation to those premises.

The original Code, which was issued in 1996, was revised in 1999 in the light of experience gained since the first duties were implemented in December 1996 and to take account of the duties imposed on service providers from 1 October 1999. This Code replaces the revised Code. It takes account of the further duties on service providers to make adjustments when the physical features of their premises make it impossible or unreasonably difficult for disabled people to use their services. Although these remaining duties do not come into force until 1 October 2004, this Code is being issued now in order to encourage service providers to be proactive and to assist them to prepare for their extended obligations.

Foreword

The Disability Rights Commission (DRC) has written and produced this Code of Practice on Part III of the Disability Discrimination Act (DDA). The Code is a revision of the consultative draft published by the DRC in May 2000 to take account of further duties under the DDA coming into force in 2004.

The DRC undertook a wide-ranging consultation on the Code involving both disabled people and service providers. The new duties upon service providers, which come into force in October 2004, were the main focus of the consultation. In response, extensive changes have been made throughout the Code. The most notable of these is the inclusion of a new chapter on the linkage between the DDA and the Building Regulations and the impact of leases. This chapter meets many of the concerns of respondents to the consultation for more detailed information in these areas.

The Code sets out our understanding of the law but there is undoubtedly some ambiguity and there are areas that will require testing in the courts. An example of this is the question of the measures service providers should take from 2004 to ensure that a physical feature is not making their service impossible or unreasonably difficult for disabled people to use. The Act sets out four possible options for service providers: removing, altering or avoiding a physical feature or providing the service by alternative means. The DDA does not prescribe what approach the service provider should use. However, the DRC believes that good practice and the most sensible approach will be to remove or alter the physical barrier to the service wherever this is possible. This is undoubtedly the most effective long term solution for both the service provider and disabled people.

The DRC has produced a range of information to help service providers in relation to their duties in 2004. This includes a Practical Guide for Small Business and Other Service Providers and some case studies. We would welcome any suggestions for further information which would be helpful.

This Code is a major tool in helping achieve the DRC's aim of 'A society where all disabled people can participate fully as equal citizens'. Making services accessible for disabled people is also good for business. I am sure that this Code will be a valuable resource in this important undertaking.

Bert Massie
Chairman, Disability Rights Commission

Contents

1
2
3
4
5
6
7
8
9
10

1 Introduction

Purpose of Part III of the Act

1.1 On 2 December 1996, the Disability Discrimination Act 1995 (the Act) brought in measures to prevent discrimination against disabled people. Part III of the Act is based on the principle that disabled people should not be discriminated against by service providers or those involved in the disposal or management of premises. Subject to limited exceptions, anyone who comes within either of these categories must comply with the duties set out in Part III. It should be noted that those selling, letting or managing premises could also have duties as service providers.

Purpose of the Code

1.2 This Code of Practice (the Code) gives practical guidance on how to prevent discrimination against disabled people in accessing services or premises. It describes the duties on those providing services to the public and those selling, letting or managing premises under Part III of the Act. The Code helps disabled people to understand the law and assists service providers, landlords and other persons to avoid complaints and litigation by adopting good practice. It also aims to advance the elimination of discrimination against disabled people and to encourage good practice.

1.3 The Disability Rights Commission (DRC) has prepared and issued this Code under the Act on the basis of a request by the Secretary of State. It applies to England, Wales and Scotland. A similar but separate Code applies to Northern Ireland.

Status of the Code

1.4 The Code does not impose legal obligations. Nor is it an authoritative statement of the law – that is a matter for the courts. However, the Code can be used in evidence in legal proceedings under the Act. Courts (and, in respect of insurance services provided to employees, employment tribunals) must take into account any part of the Code that appears to them relevant to any question arising in those proceedings. If service providers and those involved in selling, letting or managing premises follow the guidance in the Code, it may help to avoid an adverse judgement by a court in any proceedings.

How to use the Code

1.5 This chapter gives a general introduction to the Code and to Part III of the Act. **Chapters 2–8** deal with the duties on service providers, including a description of the duty to make reasonable adjustments for disabled people. **Chapter 9** deals with the duties on those selling, letting or managing premises. **Chapter 10** describes other actions made unlawful by the Act and explains what happens if discrimination is alleged.

1.6 **The Appendix** gives more information on what is meant by disability and who are disabled persons. Separate statutory guidance relating to the definition of disability has been issued under the Act (see paragraph 2.12 below).

1.7   Each chapter of the Code should be viewed as part of an overall explanation of Part III of the Act and the regulations made under it. In order to understand the law properly it is necessary to read the Code as a whole. The Code should not be read too narrowly or literally. It is intended to explain the principles of the law, to illustrate how the Act might operate in certain situations and to provide general guidance on good practice. There are some questions which the Code cannot resolve and which must await the authoritative interpretation of the courts. The Code is not intended to be a substitute for taking appropriate advice on the legal consequences of particular situations.

Examples in the Code

1.8   Examples of good practice and how the Act is likely to work are given in boxes. They are intended simply to illustrate the principles and concepts used in the legislation and should be read in that light. The examples should not be treated as complete or authoritative statements of the law.

1.9   While the examples refer to particular situations, they should be understood more widely as demonstrating how the law is likely to be applied generally. They can often be used to test how the law might apply in analogous situations involving different disabilities, services or service providers. They attempt to use as many different varieties of disabilities and services as possible to demonstrate the width and scope of the Act. References to male or female disabled people are given for realism and could, of course, apply to either sex.

References in the Code

1.10   Throughout the Code, references are made to 'service providers' for convenience. Subject to certain exceptions, Part III of the Act applies to any person or any organisation or entity which is concerned with the provision in the United Kingdom of services (including goods and facilities) to the public or a section of the public. Similarly, the Act applies to disabled people who use, or seek to use, the services so provided, whether as customers, buyers, shoppers, consumers, clients, patrons or service users.

1.11   References to the Act are shown in the margins. For example, s 1(1) means section 1(1) of the Act and Sch 1 means Schedule 1 to the Act. Where reference is made to regulations made under the Act, the Statutory Instrument number is shown in the margin (for example, SI 1996/1836).

For the most part, references to 'the Act' apply to Part III of the Disability Discrimination Act.

Changes to the legislation

1.12   This Code refers to the Disability Discrimination Act as of November 2001. There may be changes to the Act or to other legislation, for example, on transport, which may have an effect on the duties explained in this Code, and you will need to ensure that you keep up to date with any developments which may affect the Act's provisions. You can get information about this from the Disability Rights Commission (see paragraph 1.14 below for contact details).

Further information

1.13 Copies of the Act and regulations made under it (and further copies of this Code) can be purchased from the Stationery Office bookshops (see back cover). A separate Code covering the employment provisions of the Act and guidance relating to the definition of disability are also available from the same source, as is a Code dealing with the duties of trade organisations to their disabled members and applicants.

1.14 Free information about the Act can be obtained by contacting the DRC Helpline:

Telephone: _____ 08457 622 633

Faxback service: _____ 08457 622 611

Textphone: _____ 08457 622 644

The Code and information about the Act are also available in alternative formats or via the Internet [http://www.drc-gb.org].

2 What does the Act say about providing services?

Introduction

2.1 This chapter provides an overview of the provisions of Part III relating to the provision of services. It outlines what is made unlawful by the Act and explains what is meant by 'discrimination'. It describes the scope of services affected by the Act (and those which are excluded) and those people who have rights under the Act.

What does the Act make unlawful?

2.2 The Act makes it unlawful for a service provider to **discriminate** against a disabled person:

- by refusing to provide (or deliberately not providing) any service which it provides (or is prepared to provide) to members of the public; or

  s 19(1)(a)

- in the standard of service which it provides to the disabled person or the manner in which it provides it; or

  s 19(1)(c)

- in the terms on which it provides a service to the disabled person.

  s 19(1)(d)

References to providing a service include providing goods or facilities.

2.3 It is also unlawful for a service provider to **discriminate** in:

  s 19(1)(b

- failing to comply with any duty imposed on it by section 21 (a duty to make reasonable adjustments) in circumstances in which the effect of that failure is to make it impossible or unreasonably difficult for the disabled person to make use of any such service.

The reference to making use of a service includes using goods or facilities.

What does the Act mean by 'discrimination'?

2.4 The Act says that discrimination against a disabled person occurs in two possible ways.

s 20(1)

2.5 One way in which discrimination occurs is when a service provider:

- **treats the disabled person less favourably** – for a reason relating to the disabled person's disability – than it treats (or would treat) others to whom that reason does not (or would not) apply; **and**

- cannot show that the treatment is **justified.**

2.6 Making sure that a service provider does not treat a disabled person less favourably is considered in more detail in **Chapter 3** below. Whether and when a service provider might be able to justify the less favourable treatment of a disabled person is considered in **Chapter 7** below.

s 20(2)

2.7 The other way in which discrimination occurs is when a service provider:

- fails to comply with a duty imposed on it by section 21 of the Act (a duty to make **'reasonable adjustments'**) in relation to the disabled person; **and**

- cannot show that the failure is **justified.**

2.8 The duty to make reasonable adjustments is covered in greater detail in **Chapters 4, 5** and **6** below. Whether and when a service provider might be able to justify a failure to make a reasonable adjustment is considered in **Chapter 7** below.

Who has rights under the Act?

2.9 An adult or child has protection from discrimination under the Act if he or she is a disabled person. A disabled person is someone who has a physical or mental impairment which has an effect on his or her ability to carry out normal day-to-day activities. That effect must be:

- substantial (that is, more than minor or trivial); and

- adverse; and

- long term (that is, it has lasted or is likely to last for at least a year or for the rest of the life of the person affected).

2.10 Physical or mental impairment includes sensory impairments. Hidden impairments are also covered (for example, mental illness or mental health problems, learning disabilities and conditions such as diabetes or epilepsy).

In considering its duties under the Act, a service provider should not use any definition of 'disabled person' which is narrower than that in the Act.

A large supermarket has its own car park with spaces close to the entrance for use by disabled customers which are reserved for those with an orange badge car parking

ss 1-2
Schs 1–2

concession. After the introduction of the duty to make reasonable adjustments, the supermarket recognises that it must also provide appropriate assistance to all disabled people who find it unreasonably difficult to access its services and not just to those with an orange/blue badge car parking permit. For example, the supermarket also offers a carry-to-car service for disabled people who are unable to carry their shopping themselves, but who might not be orange/blue badge holders.

2.11 People who have had a disability within the terms of the Act in the past are protected from discrimination even if they no longer have the disability.

A person with a past history of mental illness, who met the definition of 'disabled person' in the Act, is turned down for travel insurance because of a blanket exclusion policy, even though she has not had any recurrence of her mental illness for many years. The provider of insurance services would be acting unlawfully under the Act unless it is able to justify the exclusion in accordance with the special rules on insurance services set out in Regulations (see **Chapter 8**).

2.12 For a fuller understanding of the concept of disability under the Act, reference should be made to the **Appendix** to this Code. A Government publication, *Guidance on matters to be taken into account in determining questions relating to the definition of disability*, provides additional help in understanding the concept of disability and in identifying disabled persons (see paragraph 1.13 above). Where relevant, the *Guidance* must be taken into account in any legal proceedings.

What services are affected by Part III of the Act?

2.13   Under the Act, the provision of services includes the provision of goods or facilities (and in this Code 'services' is used in this sense). Subject to the exclusions set out in paragraphs 2.32 to 2.37 below, the Act affects everyone concerned with the provision in the United Kingdom of services to the public, or to a section of the public, whether in the private, public or voluntary sectors. It does not matter if services are provided free (such as access to a public park) or in return for payment (for example, a meal in a restaurant).

s 19(2)

2.14   Among the services which are covered are those provided to the public by local councils, Government departments and agencies, the emergency services, charities, voluntary organisations, hotels, restaurants, pubs, post offices, banks, building societies, solicitors, accountants, telecommunications and broadcasting organisations, public utilities (such as gas, electricity and water suppliers), national parks, sports stadia, leisure centres, advice agencies, theatres, cinemas, hairdressers, shops, market stalls, petrol stations, telesales businesses, places of worship, courts, hospitals and clinics. This list is for illustration only and does not cover all the services falling under the Act.

s 19(3)

Some public bodies will be providing a service which may be covered by the Act in certain situations but not in others. For example, the police will be providing a service under the Act when giving advice and information about crime prevention, but are unlikely to be providing a service when arresting someone. A highway authority may be providing a service when assuring passage along the highway. Whether or not a function performed by a public body is a service for the purposes of the Act will depend on all the circumstances of the case.

2.15   All those involved in providing services are affected – from the most senior director or manager to the most junior employee, whether full or part-time, permanent or temporary. It does not matter whether the services in question are being provided by a sole trader, firm, company or other organisation, or whether the person involved in providing the services is self-employed or an employee, volunteer, contractor or agent.

2.16   In most cases a service provider will be providing services to a disabled person in that person's individual or personal capacity. However, sometimes a disabled person will be accessing services on behalf of an organisation (perhaps as an employee or representative of that organisation). For instance, as part of a business relationship between that organisation and the service provider, a disabled employee or representative of the organisation might have to visit parts of the service provider's premises to which a section of the public is normally admitted. The service provider is likely to owe the disabled person duties under the Act during such visits.

2.17   It is important to remember that it is the provision of the service which is affected by Part III of the Act and not the nature of the service or business or the type of establishment from which it is provided. In many cases a service provider is providing a service by a number of different means. In some cases, however, each of those means of service might be regarded as a service in itself and subject to the Act.

If a bank provides its services from temporary or mobile premises during a two week tennis tournament, those services are still covered by the Act.

A bank branch provides a cash withdrawal service over the counter from Monday to Friday during opening hours. It also provides a 24-hour cash withdrawal facility all through the week from cash machines (ATMs). To the extent that the ATM service is available when the counter service is not, the bank is likely to be providing an additional service which is subject to the duties in the Act.

A local leisure centre is subject to the Act because it provides a service to the public and not, for example, because its services are provided from a public building.

An airline company provides a flight reservation and booking service to the public on its website. This is a provision of a service and is subject to the Act.

> A television company invites members of the public to participate in a game show by telephoning its national call centre. This is the provision of a service and is subject to the Act.

s 19(3)

2.18 A wide range of services are covered by the Act so as to include access to and use of any place which members of the public are permitted to enter. For example, toilet facilities and in–store restaurants open to the public are covered and a service provider might have to make changes to entrances, fire exits and emergency escape procedures which make it impossible or unreasonably difficult for disabled people to use its service (see **Chapter 5**).

> A service provider converts a large building for use as retail premises. It recognises that it must take reasonable steps to provide a means of escape in an emergency, accessible for disabled people, which might include adjustments to the premises.

s 19(3)

2.19 The Act says that 'services' include 'access to and use of any place which members of the public are permitted to enter'. Thus, a person who permits 'members of the public' to enter such a place is providing a service to those people consisting of access to and use of that place.

2.20 Complex issues arise in the case of premises with more than one occupier, where there are common areas such as entrance halls, stairways and lifts. The Act does not expressly state whether or not the landlord (including any operator of the common parts) in such a case is a service provider for the purposes of the Act in respect of those common areas. Therefore, it does not make it explicit whether the landlord is under a duty to make reasonable adjustments to the common parts to make them accessible to disabled people.

2.21 Whether the landlord is under such an obligation is likely to depend on whether the place is one 'which members of the public are permitted to enter'. If members of the public are permitted to enter the premises, the landlord is likely to be a service provider in respect of access to the premises. If members of the public are not permitted to enter the premises, the landlord is unlikely to be a service provider under the Act.

2.22 However, the Act does not define who are 'members of the public', except to the extent that the definition of service provider refers to the provision of services to 'the public or to a section of the public'.

2.23 Members of the public are clearly permitted to enter some places. A shopping mall is an example. If the owner of a shopping mall leases shop units to individual retailers, the owner will be responsible for the common areas, such as access roads, pavements, car parks, toilets, lifts and stairs. By allowing members of the public to use these common parts, the owner is providing services to the public and is subject to the Act.

2.24 The situation of an office building with more than one occupier is not so clear. Whether the landlord is himself a service provider in respect of the common parts is likely to depend upon whether members of the public are permitted to enter the premises.

2.25 There appears to be no single test that determines whether a place is one which members of the public are permitted to enter. Whether or not a person entering the premises is a member of the public is likely to depend on all the circumstances of the case. A number of factors may be relevant, including:

- whether tenants who are service providers are actually providing services in the building rather than from the building;

- whether those admitted to the building are there for the purposes of the occupier (such as employees or maintenance and service personnel) or whether they are there for purposes of their own (such as existing or potential clients or customers); and

- the nature and extent of the security and screening arrangements in place.

2.26 Thus, a building which is normally used only by employees of the tenants is unlikely to be regarded as a place which members of the public are permitted to enter. Conversely, a building which is normally used by customers or clients of tenants may well be a place which members of the public are permitted to enter.

2.27 Because the issue is complex, landlords of premises with more than one occupier should not assume that they are not service providers for the purposes of the Act. They should anticipate that they may have responsibilities to make the common parts accessible to disabled people. They are advised to keep up to date with how the law in this respect is being interpreted.

2.28 If tenants are providing services to the public in their own right from the premises, they will have a duty under the Act to take reasonable steps to make their services accessible to disabled people (see **Chapters 4** to **6**). Where the common parts make it impossible or unreasonably difficult for disabled people to use their services, asking the landlord to make such alterations as are required in order to make the premises accessible is likely to be a reasonable step for the tenant to have to take.

2.29   If access through the common parts remains impossible or unreasonably difficult for disabled people, tenants should recognise that they may have duties themselves to provide a reasonable means of avoiding the physical feature concerned, or a reasonable alternative method of making their services available to disabled people. In any event, it makes commercial sense for service providers to anticipate the needs of their disabled customers or potential customers when determining the location of their premises, or negotiating a lease, by ensuring that the common parts of the premises they lease are accessible.

2.30   A service might appear to be provided by more than one service provider. In such a case it may be important to identify who is actually responsible for the provision of the service which has given rise to the alleged discrimination. In some cases, liability under the Act may be shared among a number of service providers.

A bank provides a cash machine facility inside a supermarket. Although the facility is located on the supermarket's premises, the service is being provided by the bank. The bank is likely to be responsible for any duties that may arise under the Act in respect of the cash machine.

However, the supermarket is likely to be responsible for ensuring that the cash machine is physically accessible to disabled customers using its premises.

An airport grants a franchise to a crèche to provide its services in a part of the airport. Although the crèche is located on the airport's premises, the service is being provided by the franchisee. The franchisee is likely to be responsible for any duties that may arise under the Act in respect of the crèche. However, access through the airport to the crèche is the responsibility of the airport.

A training company provides a non-residential conference at a hotel. The training company is responsible for any duties that may arise under the Act in respect of the conduct of the conference and the choice of an accessible venue. However, the hotel may provide some services which are part of the conference facilities, such as toilets, for which it is responsible under the Act. In addition, services provided by the hotel which are ancillary to the conference (for example, accommodation the night before the conference) are also those for which the hotel is likely to be liable under the Act.

What services are not affected?

2.31 At present Part II of the Act exempts some employers according to the number of people they employ. There are no exemptions of this kind (whether relating to size, turnover or any other factor) for service providers under Part III.

2.32 Some services are currently excluded under Part III of the Act. These are education and certain services closely related to it (see paragraphs 2.33 to 2.35 below) and the use of any means of transport (see paragraphs 2.36 and 2.37 below).

s 19(5)

Education

2.33 At present Part III of the Act specifically excludes education from the provisions relating to goods, facilities and services. Generally, primary and secondary schools, youth services and further and higher educational establishments are excluded from Part III.

s 19(5)(a)

SI 1996/1836 reg 9

Part IV of the Act currently requires schools, local education authorities, colleges and universities to provide information on access to education for disabled pupils and students.

2.34 Although education as outlined above is not covered by Part III of the Act, any other educational or training services provided to the public are likely to be subject to Part III. For example, privately-run establishments providing further education or training to the public are likely to be covered by Part III. Non-educational services which are provided by any school, college or university, whether wholly or partly to the public, are also likely to be subject to this part of the Act.

A privately-run college which provides typing courses is providing a service which is likely to be subject to Part III of the Act.

19

A parent-teacher association holds a fund-raising event in a school hall. This is a provision of a service which is likely to be subject to Part III of the Act.

A university puts on a conference which is not aimed wholly or mainly at students. Even if the majority of people who take up the places are students, the conference is still likely to be subject to Part III of the Act.

Education after 1 September 2002

2.35 The SEN and Disability Act 2001 has amended Part IV of the DDA and expanded the duties relating to disabled pupils and students. It has also removed the exemption of education from Part III of the Act, although where a Part IV duty applies, Part III cannot apply.

These new obligations will come into force in stages, beginning on 1 September 2002.

Following this implementation date, some services which had previously been excluded from Part III, and which do not fall within Part IV, are likely to be covered by Part III of the Act. This includes non-statutory youth services, such as clubs and activities run by voluntary organisations, the Scouts or church youth clubs. For further details, please see the SEN and Disability Act Code of Practice: *Schools and the SEN and Disability Act Code of Practice: Post 16 Education* (both available from the DRC Helpline).

Those educational or training services which currently fall within Part III of the Act (see paragraph 2.34 above) will continue to do so after 1 September 2002.

The use of any means of transport

2.36 Part III of the Act does not apply to any service so far as it consists of the use of any means of transport (for example, taxis, hire cars, buses, coaches, trains, aircraft and ships). However, this does not mean that transport providers are wholly exempt from Part III. They still have a duty to avoid discrimination against disabled people and to make reasonable adjustments for them in respect of matters like timetables, booking facilities, waiting rooms etc. at airports, ferry terminals and bus, coach and rail stations.

s 19(5)(b)

A wheelchair user has no protection under Part III of the Act if a ferry on which he wishes to travel is not accessible. However, if he is refused service in the buffet bar of the ferry terminal because of his disability, this is likely to be unlawful.

2.37 Part V of the Act allows the Government to set access standards for buses, coaches, trains, trams and taxis. The Government has produced regulations on access standards for rail vehicles and these apply to vehicles entering service from 1 January 1999. Regulations on access standards for certain buses and coaches, which are used on local or scheduled services, have applied to new vehicles from the end of 2000.

SI 1998/1970,
SI 2000/3318

SI 1998/2456,
SI 2000/3215

SI 2000/2990

Since April 2001 it has been unlawful for licensed taxis in England and Wales to refuse to carry, or to make any extra charge for, disabled passengers who are accompanied by a guide or assistance dog. It has also been unlawful not to allow the dog to remain with the passenger. A driver who fails to comply with this duty may be guilty of a criminal offence and subject to a fine. Similar regulations in Scotland are likely to be in place during 2002.

Services not available to the public

Private clubs

s 19(2)(b)

2.38 Services not available to the public, such as those provided by private clubs, are not covered by Part III of the Act. However, where a club does provide services to the public then the Act applies to those services.

A private golf club refuses to admit a disabled golfer to membership. This is not covered by the Act. However, if the golf club hires out its facilities for a wedding reception, the Act applies to this service. If the club allows non-members to use the course, a refusal to allow a disabled golfer to play is likely to be subject to the Act.

2.39 Private clubs are generally those where membership is a condition of participation and members have to comply with a genuine process of selection, usually by a club committee operating the club rules. Private clubs may include special interest clubs, such as a film club or cricket club, or clubs for particular groups of people, such as military or political clubs. However, simply calling a service a 'club' does not necessarily mean that the courts will consider it to be a private club. For example, commercially run businesses which may require membership – such as a health club or a video rental shop – would normally still be providing services to the public and, therefore, would be covered by the Act.

A health club in a hotel is open to the public. Club members pay an annual subscription and are provided with a membership card. Before using the club's fitness equipment, a member must undergo a fitness test. Although members have to satisfy certain requirements in order to use some of its facilities, compliance with a genuine selection procedure for membership is not a condition of using the club. The club is providing services to the public and is unlikely to be excluded from Part III of the Act.

Manufacturers and designers of products

2.40 The manufacture and design of products are not in themselves covered by Part III of the Act because they do not involve the provision of services direct to the public. Nothing in the Act requires manufacturers or designers to make changes to their products, packaging or instructions. However, it makes good business sense for manufacturers and designers to make their goods (and user information) more accessible to disabled customers and they should consider doing so as a matter of good practice.

A manufacturer of garden tools distributes its products only through high street shops. The Act does not require the manufacturer to design or market the goods so as to be easily useable by disabled purchasers.

> A food processing company produces tinned food which it supplies to a supermarket chain. Whether the tins are branded with the supermarket's own label or with that of the producer, the food processing company is not supplying goods to the public and so does not have duties under the Act. The supermarket is likely to have duties under the Act because it is supplying goods to the public, but these duties do not extend to the labelling or packaging of the tinned food.

2.41 However, if a manufacturer does provide services direct to the public, then it may have duties under the Act as a service provider.

> A manufacturer of electrical goods provides a free guarantee. A purchaser of the goods is then entitled to have the goods replaced by the manufacturer if they are faulty within 6 months of purchase. For a fixed sum the manufacturer also provides an optional extended guarantee covering the goods against defects for up to 2 years after purchase. In both cases, the manufacturer is providing a service to the public (the guarantee) and is subject to the Act in relation to the provision of that service (but not in relation to the goods themselves).

> A manufacturer of self-assembly furniture sells its products direct to the public by mail and telephone order and through a factory shop on its premises. It has duties under the Act because it is providing a service to the public. For example, it may have to make reasonable adjustments to the way in which it provides its service.

Introduction

3.1 This chapter addresses the duty of service providers to ensure that disabled people are not treated less favourably than other people when using their services. It explains what is made unlawful by the Act and what is meant by 'less favourable treatment'.

What is unlawful?

3.2 The Act says that it is unlawful for a service provider to discriminate against a disabled person by:

s 19(1)

- refusing to provide (or deliberately not providing) any service which it offers or provides to members of the public; or

  s 19(1)(a)

- providing service of a lower standard or in a worse manner; or

  s 19(1)(c)

- providing service on worse terms; or

  s 19(1)(d)

- failing to comply with a duty to make reasonable adjustments (under section 21 of the Act) if that failure has the effect of making it impossible or unreasonably difficult for the disabled person to make use of any such service.

  s 19(1)(b)

The consequences of a failure to comply with a duty to make reasonable adjustments are considered in **Chapters 4, 5** and **7**.

Less favourable treatment

3.3 A service provider discriminates against a disabled person if, for a reason which relates to the disabled person's disability, it treats the disabled person less favourably than it treats (or would treat) others to whom that reason does not (or would not) apply and it cannot show that the treatment in question is justified. This means that the treatment of the disabled person is compared with how the service provider treats (or would treat) other people to whom the reason for the treatment does not (or would not) apply. Whether and when a service provider might be able to **justify** the less favourable treatment of a disabled person is considered in **Chapter 7** below.

> A football club admits visiting supporters to its stadium. However, one visiting supporter is refused entry because he has cerebral palsy and has difficulty controlling and co-ordinating his movements. No other visiting supporter is refused entry. This would amount to less favourable treatment for a reason related to disability and, unless the football club can justify its actions, would be an unlawful refusal of service contrary to the Act.

3.4 If the treatment is caused by the fact that the person is disabled, that is treatment which 'relates to' the disability. This is the case even if some non-disabled people are also treated unfavourably for a broadly similar reason. Broadly speaking, this means that a disabled person will have been treated less favourably if he would not have received the treatment but for his disability.

A popular disco turns away prospective patrons who do not satisfy their 'image' in one respect or another. A woman with a severe facial disfigurement is not admitted by the doorman for this reason. Even though the club also does not allow entrance to many non-disabled people, for example, because it does not consider they are appropriately dressed, the woman with the severe disfigurement has been treated less favourably for a reason related to her disability. This is likely to be unlawful.

3.5 Bad treatment is not necessarily the same as less favourable treatment although, where a service provider acts unfairly or inflexibly, a court might draw inferences that discrimination has occurred.

All the supporters of a visiting team are refused entry to the stadium by the football club in the example in paragraph 3.3 above. A visiting supporter with cerebral palsy is being treated no differently from all the other visiting supporters. He has not been subjected to any less favourable treatment for a reason related to disability. However, if the football club refused entry to all the visiting supporters because one of their number has cerebral palsy, that could amount to unlawful discrimination against the disabled supporter.

3.6 The comparison can also be between the way in which one disabled person is treated compared to the way in which people with other disabilities are treated.

The football club in the example in paragraph 3.3 above refused entry to the disabled supporter with cerebral palsy. It cannot claim that it did not discriminate simply because people with other disabilities were allowed entry. The supporter with cerebral palsy has been less favourably treated in comparison with other members of the public, including the supporters with other disabilities.

3.7 A disabled person does not have to show that others were treated more favourably than they were. It is still less favourable treatment if others would have been treated better.

A party of adults with learning disabilities has exclusively booked a restaurant for a special dinner. The restaurant staff spend most of the evening making fun of the party and provide it with worse service than normal. The fact that there are no other diners in the restaurant that evening does not mean that the disabled people have not been treated less favourably than other people. Other diners would not have been treated in this way.

3.8 There must be a connection between the less favourable treatment and a reason related to the disabled person's disability.

A publican refuses to serve a disabled person whom he knows has epilepsy. He gives her no reason for refusing to serve her. Other customers in the pub are not refused service.

> A court is likely to draw an inference of discrimination in the absence of a reasonable explanation. However, if the ground for refusing her service is because she has no money, then the treatment is not for a reason which is related to the disabled person's disability.

3.9 Treating a disabled person less favourably for a reason related to his disability cannot be excused on the basis that another customer who behaved similarly (but for a reason not related to disability) would be treated in the same way.

> A group of deaf people who use British Sign Language (BSL) is refused entry to a disco. The doorman assumes that other customers might mistake communication using BSL as threatening gestures. This refusal of service is for a reason related to disability. It is likely to be unlawful even though the disco would have refused entry to any person who made similar gestures.

3.10 Nevertheless, the Act cannot be used as a pretext for disruptive or anti-social behaviour unrelated to a person's disability.

> A disco ejects a person with an artificial arm because he has drunk too much and has become abusive and disorderly. The disco would have ejected any other patron in similar circumstances. The ejection (or refusal to serve) is not for a reason related to the disabled person's disability and is unlikely to be unlawful.

Must a service provider know that a person is disabled?

3.11   A service provider may have treated a disabled person less favourably for a reason related to their disability even if it did not know the person was disabled. The test which has generally been adopted by the courts is whether, as a matter of fact, this was the reason why the disabled person was less favourably treated.

A pub employee orders a customer who is lying prone on a bench seat to leave the premises because he assumes she has had too much to drink. However, the customer is lying down as a result of a disability rather than alcoholic consumption. The refusal of further service is for 'a reason which relates to the disabled person's disability.' This will be unlawful unless the service provider is able to show that the treatment in question is justified, as defined by the Act.

3.12   As explained in **Chapter 2**, the Disability Discrimination Act only protects those who fall within the Act's definition of 'disabled person'. This definition has been the subject of developing interpretation by the courts. Moreover, some disabilities are not visible, or the extent of the impairment may be masked. It may not be practicable for service providers, or their employees, to make accurate assessments as to whether particular individuals fall within the statutory definition.

3.13   Service providers seeking to avoid discrimination, therefore, should instruct their staff that their obligations under the Act extend to everyone who falls within the definition of 'disability' and not just to those who appear to be disabled. They may also decide that it would be prudent to instruct their staff not to attempt to make a fine judgement as to whether a particular individual falls within the statutory definition, but that they should focus instead on meeting the needs of each customer.

A service provider's legal liability for its employees

3.14 Under the Act, service providers are legally responsible for the actions of their employees in the course of their employment. An employee who discriminates against a disabled customer will usually be regarded as acting in the course of their employment, even if the service provider has issued express instructions not to discriminate.

s 58(1)

3.15 However, in legal proceedings against a service provider based on the actions of an employee, it is a defence that the service provider took 'such steps as were reasonably practicable' to prevent such actions. A policy on disability which is communicated to employees is likely to be central to such a defence. It is not a defence for the service provider simply to show that the action took place without its knowledge or approval.

s 58(1), s 58(5)

What steps should a service provider consider?

3.16 Service providers are more likely to be able to comply with their duties under the Act and prevent their employees from discriminating against disabled customers if they consider the following steps:

- establishing a positive policy on the provision of services to ensure inclusion of disabled people and communicating it to all staff;

- informing all staff dealing with the public that it is unlawful to discriminate against disabled people;

- training staff to understand the service provider's policy towards disabled people, their legal obligations and the duty of reasonable adjustments;

- monitoring the implementation and effectiveness of such a policy;

- providing disability awareness and disability etiquette training for all staff who have contact with the public;

- addressing acts of disability discrimination by staff as part of disciplinary rules and procedures;

- having a customer complaints procedure which is easy for disabled people to use;

- consulting with disabled customers, disabled staff and disability organisations;

- regularly reviewing whether their services are accessible to disabled people;

- regularly reviewing the effectiveness of reasonable adjustments made for disabled people in accordance with the Act, and acting on the findings of those reviews; and

- providing regular training to staff which is relevant to the adjustments to be made.

Refusal or non-provision of service

3.17 A service provider cannot refuse to provide (or deliberately not provide) a service to a disabled person which it offers to other people, unless the refusal (or non-provision) can be justified.

s 19(1)(a)

> A party of disabled children is on a visit to a zoo. Without giving any explanation, the manager refuses to allow the children to enter the zoo. This is a refusal of a service and is likely to be unlawful.

> Bar staff in a pub pretend not to see a disabled person who is trying to be served at the bar. This is a non-provision of a service and is likely to be unlawful.

3.18 Although there is nothing unlawful about genuinely seeking to assist disabled people by informing them where they might get service more suited to their requirements, refusing to serve a disabled person may be unlawful irrespective of the intention or motive. For example, a service provider cannot refuse to serve a disabled person simply on the ground that another service provider caters better for disability-related requirements.

> An assistant in a small shop refuses to serve a disabled person, arguing that a nearby larger shop can offer a better service to disabled people. This is a refusal of service and is likely to be against the law.

33

3.19 Spurious reasons cannot be used to refuse to serve a disabled person – even if the service provider thinks that serving the disabled person will upset or raise objections from other customers.

> A disabled person with a learning disability wishes to book a hotel room. The hotel receptionist pretends that all rooms are taken in order to refuse his booking because of his disability. This is likely to be against the law.

Standard or manner of service

s 19(1)(c)

3.20 A service provider must not offer a disabled person a lower standard of service than it offers other people or serve a disabled person in a worse manner, without justification. A lower standard of service might include harassment of disabled customers or being offhand or rude towards them.

> The manager of a fast food outlet tells a person with a severe facial disfigurement that he must sit at a table out of sight of other customers, despite other tables being free. This is likely to be against the law.

> A theatre manager allots a seat with an obstructed view, despite other seats being available, to a visually impaired woman on the assumption that she would not be able to see the whole stage anyway. This is likely to be against the law.

3.21 A service provider does not have to stock special products for disabled people to avoid providing a worse standard of service (although as a matter of good practice it might consider doing so). However, if the service provider would take orders from other customers for products which it does not normally stock, it would be likely to be unlawful to refuse to take such an order from a disabled person.

A disabled customer with a visual impairment wishes to buy a large print edition of a book from a bookshop. The bookshop does not stock large print books. This is not against the law. However, the disabled customer asks the bookshop to order a large print copy of the book. If the bookshop would usually take special orders from non-disabled customers, a refusal to accept the disabled customer's order is likely to be unlawful.

Terms of service

3.22 A service provider should not provide a service to a disabled person on terms which are worse than the terms offered to other people, without justification. Worse terms include charging more for services or imposing extra conditions for using a service (but see paragraph 7.24 and 7.25 below).

s 19(1)(d)

A person who has Usher's syndrome (and who, as a consequence, is deafblind) is booking a holiday. The travel agent asks her for a larger deposit than it requires from other customers. The travel agent believes, without good reason, that because of her disability she is more likely to cancel her holiday. This is likely to be against the law.

A disabled customer who is partially sighted applies for a hire purchase loan from a finance company. The company is willing to lend to the customer, but on the condition that he should have his signature to the loan agreement witnessed by a solicitor. The company would not ask other borrowers to do this. This is likely to be unlawful.

Can service providers treat a disabled person more favourably?

3.23 The Act does not prohibit positive action in favour of disabled people (unless this would be unlawful under other legislation). Therefore, service providers may provide services on more favourable terms to a disabled person.

A cinema manager offers a better seat in the cinema without extra charge to a person with a hearing impairment who is accompanied by an assistance dog. This is to allow room for the dog. This is within the law.

A leisure park offers free entry to a communicator-guide accompanying a deafblind person. This allows the deafblind person to enjoy the park without having to pay two entrance fees. This is within the law.

4 Making changes for disabled people: the service provider's duty to make reasonable adjustments

Introduction

4.1 This chapter is concerned with the duty to make reasonable adjustments for disabled people. That duty is a cornerstone of the Act and requires service providers to take positive steps to make their services accessible to disabled people. This goes beyond simply avoiding treating disabled people less favourably for a disability-related reason.

s 21

What does the Act say?

4.2 One of the ways in which a service provider discriminates against a disabled person is where the service provider:

s 20(2)

■ fails to comply with a duty to make reasonable adjustments imposed on it in relation to the disabled person; **and**

s 20(2)(a)

■ cannot show that the failure to comply with that duty is justified.

s 20(2)(b)

Whether and when a service provider might be able to justify a failure to make a reasonable adjustment is considered in **Chapter 7** below.

4.3 It is unlawful for a service provider to discriminate in this way if the effect is to make it impossible or unreasonably difficult for the disabled person to make use of services which the service provider offers to the public.

s 19(1)(b)

4.4 As explained in paragraphs 3.14 and 3.15 above, under the Act service providers are legally responsible for the actions of their employees in the course of their employment. An employee who discriminates against a disabled customer will usually be regarded as acting in the course of their employment. This applies equally in respect of a failure by a service provider's employees to comply with the duty to make reasonable adjustments.

What is the duty to make reasonable adjustments?

s 21

4.5 Where a service provider offers services to the public, it has a legal duty to take such steps as it is reasonable for the service provider to have to take in all the circumstances of the case in the situations described below. This duty is referred to in this Code as the duty to make reasonable adjustments.

4.6 The duty to make reasonable adjustments comprises a series of duties falling into three main areas:

- changing practices, policies and procedures;

- providing auxiliary aids and services;

- overcoming a physical feature by

  - removing the feature; or

  - altering it; or

  - avoiding it; or

  - providing services by alternative methods.

The duties are being introduced in two stages.

4.7 From 1 October 1999, a service provider has had to take reasonable steps to:

- **change a practice, policy or procedure** which makes it impossible or unreasonably difficult for disabled people to make use of its services; **s 21(1)**

- provide an **auxiliary aid or service** if it would enable (or make it easier for) disabled people to make use of its services; **s 21(4)**

- provide a reasonable **alternative method** of making its services available to disabled people where a **physical feature** makes it impossible or unreasonably difficult for disabled people to make use of the services. **s 21(2)(d)**

4.8 From **1 October 2004**, where a **physical feature** makes it impossible or unreasonably difficult for disabled people to make use of services, a service provider will have to take reasonable steps to:

- **remove** the feature; or **s 21(2)(a)**

- **alter** it so that it no longer has that effect; or **s 21(2)(b)**

- provide a reasonable means of **avoiding** it; or **s 21(2)(c)**

- provide a reasonable alternative method of making the services available (see paragraph 4.6 above). **s 21(2)(d)**

It makes sense for service providers to plan ahead by taking any opportunities which arise, or bringing forward plans, to make alterations to their premises to benefit disabled people before 2004. Structural or other physical changes will not be required before 1 October 2004 (but might be made before that date; see paragraphs 5.33 to 5.35 below). Examples of these are: widening a doorway; providing a permanent ramp for a wheelchair user; relocating light switches, door handles or shelves for someone who has difficulty in reaching; providing appropriate contrast in decor to assist the safe mobility of a visually impaired person; installing a permanent induction loop system; providing tactile buttons in lifts.

General approach to making reasonable adjustments

4.9 It is important that service providers do not assume that the only way to make services accessible to disabled people is to make a physical alteration to their premises (such as installing a ramp or widening a doorway). Often, minor measures such as allowing more time to serve a disabled customer, will help disabled people to use a service. Disability awareness training for staff is also likely to be appropriate. However, adjustments in the form of physical alterations may be the only answer if other measures are not sufficient to overcome barriers to access.

4.10 A service provider should be able to identify the more obvious physical or other barriers or impediments to access by disabled people to its services. Regularly reviewing the way in which it provides its services to the public, for example via periodic disability audits, might help a service provider identify any less obvious or unintentional barriers to access for disabled people. Obtaining the views of disabled customers and disabled employees will also assist a service provider. Disabled people know best what hurdles they face in trying to use the services provided. They can identify difficulties in accessing services and might also suggest solutions involving the provision of reasonable adjustments. In addition, local and national disability groups or organisations of disabled people have extensive experience which service providers can draw on. Listening carefully and responding to what disabled people really want helps service providers find the best way of meeting disabled people's requirements and expectations.

4.11 Employee training is also an important factor in providing reasonable adjustments. Employees should be generally aware of the requirements of disabled customers and potential customers and should appreciate how to respond appropriately to requests for a reasonable adjustment. They should know how to provide an auxiliary service and how to use any auxiliary aids which the service provider offers. Employees could also be encouraged to acquire additional skills in serving disabled people; for example, communicating with hearing impaired people and those with speech impairments.

Use of reasonable adjustment examples

4.12 Section 21 of the Act refers to such steps as it is reasonable, in all the circumstances of the case, for the service provider 'to have to take' to make its services accessible to disabled people. The examples in this Code use the same language by discussing whether the step in the example concerned is likely to be a reasonable step for the service provider 'to have to take'. This is not intended to indicate that the step considered in the example is the only way in which the service provider can meet its duty under the Act. In any particular case, the service provider's duty to make reasonable adjustments might be discharged by taking a different step or steps.

s 21(1)

To whom is the duty to make reasonable adjustments owed?

4.13 A service provider's duty to make reasonable adjustments is a duty owed to disabled people at large. It is not simply a duty that is weighed up in relation to each individual disabled person who wants to access a service provider's services. Disabled people are a diverse group with different requirements which service providers need to consider.

At what point does the duty to make reasonable adjustments arise?

4.14 Service providers should not wait until a disabled person wants to use a service which they provide before they give consideration to their duty to make reasonable adjustments. They should be thinking now about the accessibility of their services to disabled people. Service providers should be planning continually for the reasonable adjustments they need to make, whether or not they already have disabled customers. They should anticipate the requirements of disabled people and the adjustments that may have to be made for them. In many cases, it is appropriate to ask customers to identify whether they have any particular requirements and, if so, what adjustments may need to be made. Failure to anticipate the need for an adjustment may render it too late to comply with the duty to make the adjustment. Furthermore, it may not of itself provide a defence to a claim that it was reasonable to have provided one.

An invitation to the public to make submissions and to attend a public inquiry indicates that any reasonable adjustments will be made on request if this will assist disabled people to make submissions or to attend the inquiry. This helps to ensure that the public inquiry is accessible.

Does the duty of reasonable adjustment apply even if the service provider does not know that the person is disabled?

4.15 A service provider owes a duty of reasonable adjustment to 'disabled persons' as defined by the Act. This is a duty to disabled people at large, and applies regardless of whether the service provider knows that a particular member of the public is disabled or whether it currently has disabled customers.

4.16 For this reason, employees should be made aware that they may be discriminating unlawfully even if they do not know that a customer is disabled and they should be reminded that not all impairments are visible. As explained in this chapter and in **Chapters 3** and **5**, the duty of reasonable adjustment is best met by the service provider trying to anticipate the types of problems which could arise, and by training its employees to enquire rather than act on assumptions. The aim should be that, when disabled customers request services, the service provider has already taken all reasonable steps to ensure that they can be served without being put to unreasonable difficulty.

Must service providers anticipate every barrier?

4.17 When considering the provision of a reasonable adjustment, a service provider should be flexible in its approach. However, there may be situations where it is not reasonable for a service provider to anticipate a particular requirement.

4.18 Once a service provider has become aware of the requirements of a particular disabled person who uses or seeks to use its services, it might then become reasonable for the service provider to take a particular step to meet these requirements. This is especially so where a disabled person has pointed out the difficulty which he or she faces in accessing services, or has suggested a reasonable solution to that difficulty.

How long does the duty continue?

4.19 The duty to make reasonable adjustments is a continuing duty. Service providers should keep the duty under regular review in the light of their experience with disabled people wanting to access their services. In this respect it is an evolving duty, and not something that needs simply to be considered once and once only, and then forgotten. What was originally a reasonable step to take might no longer be sufficient and the provision of further or different adjustments might then have to be considered.

A large sports complex amends its 'no dogs' policy to allow entry to guide dogs. It offers guide dog users a tour of the complex to acquaint them with routes. This is likely to be a reasonable step for it to have to take at this stage. However, the complex then starts building work and this encroaches on paths within the complex, making it difficult for guide dog users to negotiate their way around. Offering an initial tour is therefore no longer an effective adjustment as it does not make the complex accessible to guide dog users. The service provider therefore decides to offer guide dog users appropriate additional assistance from staff whilst the building work is being undertaken. This is likely to be a reasonable step for the service provider to have to take in the circumstances then existing.

4.20 Equally, a step which might previously have been an unreasonable one for a service provider to have to take could subsequently become a reasonable step in the light of changed circumstances. For example, technological developments may provide new or better solutions to the problems of inaccessible services.

A library has a small number of computers for the public to use. When the computers were originally installed, the library investigated the option of incorporating text to speech software for people with a visual impairment. It rejected the option because the software was very expensive and not particularly effective. It would not have been a reasonable step for the library to have to take at that stage. The library proposes to replace the computers. It makes enquiries and establishes that text to speech software is now efficient and within the library's budget. The library decides to install the software on the replacement computers. This is likely to be a reasonable step for the library to have to take at this time.

What is meant by 'reasonable steps'?

4.21 Section 21 refers to a service provider being under a duty to take such steps as it is reasonable, in all the circumstances of the case, for it to have to take in order to make reasonable adjustments. The Act does not specify that any particular factors should be taken into account. What is a reasonable step for a particular service provider to have to take depends on all the circumstances of the case. It will vary according to:

- the type of services being provided;

- the nature of the service provider and its size and resources;

- the effect of the disability on the individual disabled person.

4.22 However, without intending to be exhaustive, the following are some of the factors which might be taken into account when considering what is reasonable:

- whether taking any particular steps would be effective in overcoming the difficulty that disabled people face in accessing the services in question;

- the extent to which it is practicable for the service provider to take the steps;

- the financial and other costs of making the adjustment;

- the extent of any disruption which taking the steps would cause;

- the extent of the service provider's financial and other resources;

- the amount of any resources already spent on making adjustments;

- the availability of financial or other assistance.

Customers in a busy post office are served by staff at a counter after queuing in line. A disabled customer with severe arthritis wishes to purchase a TV licence. He experiences great pain if he has to stand for more than a couple of minutes. Other customers would not expect to have to undergo similar discomfort in order to buy a TV licence. Thus, the post office's queuing policy makes it unreasonably difficult for the disabled person to use the service. Consideration will have to be given to how the queuing policy could be adjusted so as to accommodate the requirements of such disabled customers.

The post office staff could ask the customer to take a seat and then serve him in the same way as if he had queued. Alternatively, it might provide a separate service desk with seating for disabled customers. Depending on the size of the post office, these might be reasonable steps to have to take to adjust the queuing policy. However, it is not likely to be a reasonable step for the post office to send a member of staff to the disabled customer's home in order to sell him the TV licence. The time and expense involved would probably be an unreasonable use of the post office's resources, particularly in proportion to the degree of benefit to the disabled customer.

4.23 It is more likely to be reasonable for a service provider with substantial financial resources to have to make an adjustment with a significant cost than for a service provider with fewer resources. The resources available to the service provider as a whole are likely to be taken into account as well as other calls on those resources. Where the resources of the service provider are spread across more than one business unit or profit centre, the calls on them all are likely to be taken into account in assessing reasonableness.

A small retailer has two shops within close proximity to each other. It has conducted an audit to identify what adjustments for disabled people will be needed. At one of its shops, customers with mobility impairments cannot use all the services provided. The other shop can be easily reached by such customers and offers the same services, all of which are accessible to disabled people. Although the retailer originally hoped to make its services in both shops equally accessible, it is constrained by its limited resources. Therefore, for the present, it decides not to make all the services at the first shop accessible to customers with mobility impairments. In these circumstances, it is unlikely to be in breach of the Act.

4.24 Service providers should bear in mind that there are no hard and fast solutions. Action which may result in reasonable access to services being achieved for some disabled people may not necessarily do so for others. Equally, it is not enough for service providers to make some changes if they still leave their services impossible or unreasonably difficult for disabled people to use.

The organiser of a large public conference provides qualified British Sign Language (BSL) interpreters to enable deaf delegates to follow and participate in the conference. However, this does not assist delegates with a mobility impairment or visual disabilities to access the conference, nor does it help delegates with a hearing impairment who do not use BSL but who can lipread. The conference organiser will need to consider the requirements of these delegates also.

4.25 Similarly, a service provider will not have taken reasonable steps if it attempts to provide an auxiliary aid or service which in practice does not help disabled people to access the service provider's services. The way in which an auxiliary aid or service is provided may be just as important as the auxiliary aid or service itself.

Despite providing qualified British Sign Language (BSL) interpreters for deaf delegates who use BSL, the conference organiser fails to ensure that those delegates have the option to be seated near and in full view of the interpreters (who are themselves in a well-lit area). As a result, not all those delegates are able to follow the interpretation. The auxiliary service provided has not been effective in making the conference fully accessible to those deaf delegates.

4.26 Once a service provider has decided to put a reasonable adjustment in place, it is important to draw its existence to the attention of disabled people. The service provider should also establish a means for letting disabled people know about the adjustment where the service is otherwise likely to be unreasonably difficult to use. This might be done by a simple sign or notice at the entrance to the service provider's premises or at a service point. Alternatively, the availability of a reasonable adjustment might be highlighted in forms or documents used by the service provider, such as publicity materials. In all cases, it is important to use a means of communication which is itself accessible to disabled people.

An airport provides transfer by electric buggy between terminals and gates for passengers with a mobility impairment. Prominent signs at the entrance to the arrivals and departures halls and at check-in desks assist disabled passengers in accessing that auxiliary service.

A hospital has its forms and explanatory literature in accessible alternative formats such as large print, audio tape and braille. A prominent note to that effect on the literature sent to patients, or a specific mention of this by reception staff when a patient first visits the hospital, assists disabled patients to access the service.

4.27 If, having considered the issue thoroughly, there are genuinely no steps that it would be reasonable for a service provider to take to make its services accessible, the service provider is unlikely to be in breach of the law if it makes no changes. Such a situation is likely to be rare.

Protecting the fundamental nature of a business or service

4.28 The Act does not require a service provider to take any steps which would fundamentally alter the nature of its service, trade, profession or business. This means that a service provider does not have to comply with a duty to make reasonable adjustments in a way which would so alter the nature of its business that the service provider would effectively be providing a completely different kind of service.

s 21(6)

> A restaurant refuses to deliver a meal to the home of a disabled person with severe agoraphobia (a fear of public or open spaces) on the grounds that this would result in the provision of a different kind of service. This is unlikely to be against the law. However, if the restaurant already provides a home delivery service, it is likely to be discriminatory to refuse to serve the disabled person in this way.

> A night club with low level lighting is not required to adjust the lighting to accommodate customers who are partially sighted if this would fundamentally change the atmosphere or ambience of the club.

> A hair and beauty salon provides appointments to clients at its premises in a town centre. A disabled person with a respiratory impairment is unable to travel into town because this exacerbates her disability. She asks the salon to provide her with an appointment at home.

> The salon refuses as it does not provide a home appointment service to any of its clients. This is likely to be within the law.

4.29 However, there might be an alternative reasonable adjustment which would ensure the accessibility of the services. If this can be provided without fundamentally altering the nature of the services or business, it would be a reasonable step for the service provider to have to take.

Cost of providing reasonable adjustments

s.20(5)

4.30 The Act does not allow a service provider to pass on the additional costs of complying with the duty to make reasonable adjustments to disabled customers alone. The costs of providing reasonable adjustments are part of the service providers' general expenses.

> A guest house has installed an audio-visual fire alarm in one of its guest bedrooms in order to accommodate visitors with a sensory impairment. In order to recover the costs of this installation, the landlady charges disabled guests a higher daily charge for that room, although it is otherwise identical to other bedrooms. This is unlikely to be within the law.

s 20(5)

4.31 Sometimes a service provider makes an additional service available to customers for which there is a charge. If the additional service is itself a reasonable adjustment which the service provider has to provide under the Act to its disabled customers, those disabled customers cannot be charged for that service.

A wine merchant runs an online shopping service and charges all customers for home delivery. Its customers include disabled people with mobility impairments. Since this online service is not impossible or unreasonably difficult for disabled people with mobility impairments to use, home delivery, in these circumstances, will not be a reasonable adjustment that the wine merchant has to make under the Act. Therefore, the wine merchant can charge disabled customers in the same way as other customers for this service.

However, another wine merchant has a shop which is inaccessible to disabled people with mobility impairments. Home delivery in these circumstances might be a reasonable adjustment for the wine merchant to have to make for such customers. The wine merchant could not then charge such customers for home delivery, even though it charges other customers for home delivery.

What is 'unreasonably difficult'?

4.32   It is unlawful for a service provider to discriminate against a disabled person in failing to comply with a duty to make reasonable adjustments when the effect of that failure is to make it impossible or 'unreasonably difficult' for the disabled person to make use of services provided to the public. The Act does not define what is meant by 'unreasonably difficult'.

4.33   However, when considering if services are unreasonably difficult for disabled people to use, service providers should take account of whether the time, inconvenience, effort, discomfort or loss of dignity entailed in using

s 19(1)(b)

the service would be considered unreasonable by other people if they had to endure similar difficulties (see the example at paragraph 4.22 above).

What happens if the duty to make reasonable adjustments is not complied with?

s 19(1)(b)

s 20(2)

s 21(10)

4.34 A service provider must comply with the duty to make reasonable adjustments in order to avoid committing an act of unlawful discrimination. A disabled person is able to make a claim against a service provider if:

- the service provider fails to do what is required; and

- that failure makes it impossible or unreasonably difficult for that disabled person to access any services provided by the service provider to the public; and

- the service provider cannot show that such a failure is justified in relation to the disabled person.

5 Reasonable adjustments in practice

Introduction

5.1 In **Chapter 4** the Code outlines the concept of the duty to make reasonable adjustments and provides an overview of the legal principles which underpin it. In this chapter the Code explains and illustrates how the duty works in practice.

5.2 As explained in **Chapter 4**, the duty to make reasonable adjustments comprises a series of duties falling into three main areas:

- changing practices, policies and procedures;

- providing auxiliary aids and services;

- overcoming a physical feature by

  - removing the feature; or

  - altering it; or

  - providing a reasonable means of avoiding it; or

  - providing the service by a reasonable alternative method.

A physical feature includes, for example, a feature arising from the design or construction of a building or the approach or access to premises (and see paragraph 5.44 below).

5.3 These duties are being introduced in two stages.

Since 1 October 1999 the duties in respect of:

- changing practices, policies and procedures;

- providing auxiliary aids and services;

- overcoming a physical feature by providing services by reasonable alternative methods, have been in force.

From 1 October 2004 the duties in respect of:

- overcoming a physical feature by

  - removing the feature; or

  - altering it; or

  - providing a reasonable means of avoiding it, will also apply.

This chapter considers each in turn.

Practices, policies and procedures

What is the duty to change a practice, policy or procedure?

5.4 When a service provider is providing services to its customers, it will have established a particular way of doing this. Its practices (including policies and procedures) may be set out formally or may have become established informally or by custom. A service provider might have a practice which – perhaps unintentionally – makes it impossible or unreasonably difficult for disabled people to make use of its services.

5.5 In such a case, the service provider must take such steps as it is reasonable for it to have to take, in all the circumstances, to change the practice so that it no longer has that effect. This may simply mean instructing staff to waive a practice or amending a policy to allow exceptions or abandoning it altogether. Often, such a change involves little more than an extension of the courtesies which most service providers already show to their customers.

> A restaurant has a policy of refusing entry to male diners who do not wear a collar and tie. A disabled man who wishes to dine in the restaurant is unable to wear a tie because he has psoriasis (a severe skin complaint) of the face and neck. Unless the restaurant is prepared to waive its policy, its effect is to exclude the disabled customer from the restaurant. This is likely to be unlawful.

> A video rental shop allows only people who can provide a driving licence as proof of their identity to become members. This automatically excludes some disabled people from joining because the nature of their disabilities prevents them from obtaining a driving licence (for example blind people or some people with epilepsy or mental health problems). The shop would be required to take reasonable steps to change this practice. It does so by being prepared to accept alternative forms of identification from its customers. This is likely to be a reasonable step for the shop to have to take.

What are practices, policies and procedures?

5.6 Practices, policies and procedures relate to the way in which a service provider operates its business or provides its services. This includes any requirements that it makes of its customers. In principle, the terms cover:

- what a service provider actually does (its **practice**);

- what a service provider intends to do (its **policy**);

- how a service provider plans to go about it (its **procedure**).

However, the three terms overlap and it is not always sensible to treat them as separate concepts.

A DIY superstore has a policy of not allowing dogs onto its premises. Members of staff are instructed to prevent anyone with a dog from entering the superstore. The 'no dogs' policy is enforced in practice by this procedure. The policy makes it unreasonably difficult for disabled people accompanied by a guide or assistance dog to use the DIY superstore. The superstore has a duty to take such steps as are reasonable for it to have to take to avoid that effect and to make its services accessible to disabled people. It decides to amend its 'no dogs' policy by allowing an exception for disabled people accompanied by a guide or assistance dog. This is likely to be a reasonable step for the superstore to have to take.

What are 'reasonable steps' in relation to practices, policies and procedures?

5.7   The Act does not define what are 'reasonable steps' for a service provider to have to take in order to change its practices. The kinds of factors which may be relevant are described in paragraphs 4.21 to 4.27 above.

5.8   The purpose of taking the steps is to ensure that the practice no longer has the effect of making it impossible or unreasonably difficult for disabled people to use a service. Where there is an adjustment that the service provider could reasonably put in place and which would make the service accessible, it is not sufficient for the service provider to take some lesser step which would not result in the service being accessible.

A medium-sized supermarket installs one extra-wide check-out lane intending it to be available to customers who are wheelchair users or accompanied by infants. However, that check-out lane is also designated as an express lane available only to shoppers with 10 or less items. The effect of this practice is to exclude wheelchair-users from taking advantage of the accessible check-out unless they are making only a few purchases. It is likely to be a reasonable step for the supermarket to have to take to amend its practice by designating another check-out lane as the express lane.

5.9   A practice may have the effect of excluding or screening out disabled people from enjoying access to services. Or the practice may create a barrier or hurdle which makes it unreasonably difficult for disabled people to access the services. In such cases, unless the practice can be justified, a reasonable step for a service provider to have to take might be to abandon it entirely or to amend or modify it so that it no longer has that effect.

A town hall has procedures for the evacuation of the building in the event of a fire or emergency. Visitors are required to leave the building by designated routes. The emergency procedures are part of the way in which the town hall provides services to its visitors. It modifies the procedures (with the agreement of the local fire authority) to allow visitors with mobility impairments or sensory disabilities to be evacuated safely. This is likely to be a reasonable step for the town hall to have to take.

A hotel refurbishes a number of rooms on each floor which are fully accessible to disabled guests. However, the hotel's reservations system allocates rooms on a first come, first served basis as guests arrive and register. The effect is that on some occasions the specially refurbished rooms are allocated to non- disabled guests and late-arriving disabled guests cannot be accommodated in those rooms. The hotel decides to change its reservation policy so that the accessible rooms are either reserved for disabled guests in advance or are allocated last of all. This is likely to be a reasonable step for the hotel to have to take.

Auxiliary aids and services

What is the duty to provide auxiliary aids or services?

5.10   A service provider must take reasonable steps to provide auxiliary aids or services if this would enable (or make it easier for) disabled people to make use of any services which it offers to the public.

s 21(4)

What is an auxiliary aid or service?

5.11   The Act gives two examples of auxiliary aids or services: the provision of information on audio tape and the provision of a sign language interpreter.

s 21(4)

A building society provides information on an audio tape about its savings accounts. A customer with a visual impairment can use the audio tape at home or in a branch to decide whether to open an account. This is an auxiliary aid.

A department store has a member of staff able to communicate with deaf clients who use British Sign Language. This is an auxiliary service.

5.12   But these are only illustrations of the kinds of auxiliary aids or services which a service provider might need to consider. An auxiliary aid or service might be the provision of a special piece of equipment or simply extra assistance to disabled people from (perhaps specially trained) staff. In some cases a technological solution might be available.

A large supermarket provides specially designed shopping baskets and trolleys which can be easily used by disabled shoppers in a wheelchair or with reduced mobility. It also provides electronic hand-held bar code readers with synthesised voice output which helps customers with a visual impairment to identify goods and prices. These are auxiliary aids which enable disabled shoppers to use the supermarket's services.

Disabled customers with a visual impairment or a learning disability may need assistance in a large supermarket to locate items on their shopping list. The supermarket instructs one of its employees to find the items for them. The supermarket is providing an auxiliary service which makes its goods accessible.

A petrol station decides that an assistant will help disabled people use the petrol pumps on request. It places a prominent notice at the pumps advertising this. This is an auxiliary service.

5.13 In any event, service providers should ensure that any auxiliary aids they provide are carefully chosen and properly maintained.

A person with a hearing impairment is attending a performance at a theatre. When booking the tickets he is told that the theatre auditorium has an induction loop. However, the theatre does not check that the loop is working and on the day of the performance the system is not working properly. Although the theatre has provided an auxiliary aid, its failure to check that the loop is working properly means that the theatre is unlikely to have taken reasonable steps to enable disabled people to make use of its services.

5.14 What is an appropriate auxiliary aid or service will vary according to the type of service provider, the nature of the services being provided, and the requirements of the disabled customers or potential customers. Auxiliary aids and services are not limited to aids to communication.

A community centre is accessible by two raised steps. It provides a suitably chosen portable ramp which helps disabled people with a mobility impairment to enter the premises safely. This is an auxiliary aid which is suited to the requirements of those people.

A new cinema complex has deep airline-style seats. A disabled patron with restricted growth finds it difficult to see the screen when using such a seat. The cinema provides a bolster cushion on request which enables him to enjoy the film. This is an auxiliary aid appropriate to the circumstances.

> A museum provides a written guide to its exhibits. It wants to make the exhibits accessible to visitors with learning disabilities. The museum produces a version of the guide which uses plain language, text and pictures to explain the exhibits. This is an auxiliary aid suited to visitors with learning disabilities and may also benefit other people.

s 21(4)
SI 1999/1191
reg 4

5.15 From 1 October 2004 auxiliary aids and services could be any kind of aid or service (whether temporary or permanent). Until 1 October 2004 the Disability Discrimination (Services and Premises) Regulations 1999 temporarily restrict their meaning so as not to require the provision of auxiliary aids or services which involve a permanent alteration to the physical fabric of premises (or fixtures, fittings, furnishings, furniture, equipment or materials). There is nothing in the Act, however, to prevent such provision in anticipation of 1 October 2004 and service providers should take note of paragraphs 5.33 to 5.35 below.

5.16 Nothing in the Act requires a service provider to provide an auxiliary aid or service to be used for personal purposes unconnected to the services being provided or to be taken away by the disabled person after use.

> A solicitors' firm lends an audio tape recorder to a client with multiple disabilities who is unable to communicate in writing or to attend the firm's office. The client uses this auxiliary aid in order to record his instructions or witness statement. The client would be expected to return the recorder after use.

What are 'reasonable steps' in relation to auxiliary aids or services?

5.17 The duty to provide auxiliary aids or services requires the service provider to take such steps as it is reasonable for it to have to take in all the circumstances of the case to make its services accessible to disabled people. What might be reasonable for a large service provider (or one with substantial resources) might not be reasonable for a smaller service provider. The size of the service provider, the resources available to it and the cost of the auxiliary service are relevant factors.

A large national museum has hourly guided tours of a popular major exhibition. It provides a radio microphone system for hearing aid users to accompany the tour and on one day a week has a BSL interpreter available. The museum advertises this service and encourages BSL users to book space with the interpreter on the tours on that day. These are likely to be reasonable steps for the museum to have to take.

A small, private museum with limited resources provides a daily guided tour of its exhibits. It investigates the provision of equipment for hearing aid users such as an induction loop in the main gallery or a radio microphone system to accompany the tour, but, after careful consideration, it rejects both options as too expensive and impracticable. Instead, with little effort or cost, the museum decides to provide good quality audio taped guides (with an option of plug-in neck loops) which can be used by people with hearing aids who want to follow the guided tour. This is likely to be a reasonable step for the museum to have to take.

5.18 The reasonableness of the service provider's response to disabled people's requirements will inevitably vary with the circumstances. The kinds of factors which may be relevant are described in paragraphs 4.21 to 4.27 above.

A hospital physiotherapist has a new patient who uses BSL as his main means of communication. The hospital arranges for a qualified BSL interpreter to be present at the initial assessment, which requires a good level of communication on both sides. At this initial assessment the physiotherapist and the disabled patient also discuss what other forms of communication services or aids would be suitable. They agree that for major assessments a BSL interpreter will be used but that at routine treatment appointments they will communicate with a notepad and pen. This is because these appointments do not require the same level or intensity of communication. This is likely to be a reasonable step for the hospital to have to take.

5.19 For a deaf person who uses British Sign Language as his or her main form of communication, having a qualified BSL interpreter is the most effective method of communication. This is because for people whose first language is BSL (rather than spoken or written English) exchange of written notes or lipreading can be an uncertain means of communication.

British Sign Language Interpretation may not be easily available and should be arranged in advance wherever possible. If an interpreter is not available, the service provider should consider an alternative method of communication, in consultation with the deaf person.

5.20 A service provider will have to consider what steps it can reasonably take to meet the individual requirements of disabled people. How effectively the service provider is able to do so will depend largely on how far it has anticipated the requirements of its disabled customers. Many things that seem impossible at the time they are confronted might have been accommodated relatively easily if prior thought had been given to the question.

5.21 The Act leaves open what particular auxiliary aids or services might be provided in specific circumstances. Disabled people may be able to help the service provider to identify difficulties in accessing the service and what kind of auxiliary aid or service will overcome them. It is good practice to include disabled customers in the process of considering what reasonable adjustments should be made. However the duty remains on the service provider to determine what steps it needs to take.

Using auxiliary aids or services to improve communication

5.22 In many cases, a service provider will need to consider providing auxiliary aids or services to improve communication with people with a sensory impairment (such as those affecting hearing or sight) or a speech impairment or learning disabilities. The type of auxiliary aid or service will vary according to the importance, length, complexity or frequency of the communication involved. In some cases, more than one type of auxiliary aid or service might be appropriate, as different people have different communication requirements. Account should also be taken of people with multiple communication disabilities, such as deaf-blindness or combined speech and hearing disabilities.

A cinema offers patrons a telephone booking service. Its booking office installs a textphone and trains its staff to use it. This offers access to deaf patrons and is likely to be a reasonable step for the cinema to have to take.

The booking office of a small heritage railway decides to communicate with passengers who have speech or hearing impairments by exchanging written notes. This is likely to be a reasonable step for this service provider to have to take.

However, it is unlikely to be a sufficient reasonable adjustment for the booking office at a mainline rail terminus to make for such passengers. Instead, it installs an induction loop system and a textphone. These are likely to be reasonable steps for a large station to have to take.

Provision for people with a hearing disability

5.23   For people with hearing disabilities, the range of auxiliary aids or services which it might be reasonable to provide to ensure that services are accessible might include one or more of the following:

- written information (such as a leaflet or guide);

- a facility for taking and exchanging written notes;

- a verbatim speech-to-text transcription service;

- induction loop systems;

- subtitles;

- videos with BSL interpretation;

- information displayed on a computer screen;

- accessible websites;

- textphones, telephone amplifiers and inductive couplers;

- teletext displays;

- audio-visual telephones;

- audio-visual fire alarms;

- qualified BSL interpreters or lipspeakers.

A deaf defendant (or defender) in court proceedings uses BSL as his main form of communication. The court arranges for a qualified BSL interpreter to interpret and voice over his evidence in court. This is likely to be a reasonable step for the court to have to take.

A hearing impaired person who lipreads as her main form of communication wants a secured loan from a bank. In the initial stages it might be reasonable for the bank to communicate with her by providing printed literature or information displayed on a computer screen.

However, before a secured loan agreement is signed, this particular bank usually provides a borrower with an oral explanation of its contents. At that stage it is likely to be reasonable, with the customer's consent, for the bank to arrange for a qualified lipspeaker to be present so that any complex aspects of the agreement can be fully explained and communicated.

A television broadcasting company provides teletext sub-titles to some of its programmes. This allows viewers with a hearing impairment to follow the programmes more easily. This is likely to be a reasonable step for the broadcasting company to have to take.

5.24 Where sign language interpretation is used as an auxiliary service the interpreter should be capable of communicating accurately and efficiently with both the disabled person and the other parties involved. Other interpretation services such as lipspeakers and Makaton communicators should similarly be capable of communicating accurately and effectively.

5.25 Service providers should bear in mind that hearing impairments take many forms and are of varying degrees. What might be a reasonable auxiliary aid or service for a person with tinnitus or reduced hearing might not be a reasonable adjustment for someone who is profoundly deaf.

A bus station fits an induction loop system at its booking office. This ensures that customers who have reduced hearing and use hearing aids are able to communicate effectively with the booking office. However, this does not help profoundly deaf customers. The bus company instructs its staff to take time to communicate by using a pen and notepad to discover what the customer wants and to give information. The staff are also trained to speak looking directly at the customer to allow those customers who can lipread to do so. These are likely to be reasonable steps for the bus station to have to take.

Provision for people with a visual impairment

5.26   For people with visual impairments, the range of auxiliary aids or services which it might be reasonable to provide to ensure that services are accessible might include one or more of the following:

- readers;

- documents in large or clear print, Moon or braille;

- information on computer disk or e-mail;

- information on audiotape;

- telephone services to supplement other information;

- spoken announcements or verbal communication;

- accessible websites;

- assistance with guiding;

- audiodescription services;

- large print or tactile maps/plans and three-dimensional models;

- touch facilities (for example, interactive exhibits in a museum or gallery).

A restaurant changes its menus daily. For that reason it considers it is not practicable to provide menus in alternative formats, such as braille. However, its staff spend a little time reading out the menu for blind customers and the restaurant ensures that there is a large print copy available. These are likely to be reasonable steps for the restaurant to have to take.

A utility company supplying gas and electricity to domestic customers sends out quarterly bills. On request, the company is willing to provide the bills in alternative formats such as braille or large print for customers with visual impairments. This is likely to be a reasonable step for the utility company to have to take.

Every year a local council sends out information to local residents about new council tax rates. Because the information is important, the council provides copies in large print. On request, it is also prepared to supply the information in alternative media such as braille or audiotape or to explain the new rates to individual residents with visual impairments. These are likely to be reasonable steps for the council to have to take.

A customer with a visual impairment wishes to buy a compact disc player from a small specialist hi-fi shop. The shop arranges for a member of staff to assist the customer by reading out product details, packaging information or prices. This is likely to be a reasonable step for the shop to have to take.

5.27 As with other forms of sensory impairments, visual disabilities are of varying kinds and degrees. Service providers need to consider what is the most appropriate auxiliary aid or service to provide. More than one auxiliary aid or service may be necessary according to the circumstances.

A small estate agent is reviewing the accessibility of its sales literature for clients who are partially sighted or blind. Because of the nature of the service it provides and the size of its business, the estate agent concludes that it is not practicable to make particulars of houses for sale available in braille. However, the estate agent decides to change the print size and redesign the appearance of its written sales particulars. This makes the estate agent's sales information more accessible to its partially sighted clients, but does not assist those who are blind. It therefore also decides to put the information on audio tape on request. These are likely to be reasonable steps for the estate agent to have to take.

A housing benefit office ensures that claim forms and information literature are available in large print for partially sighted claimants. It also arranges for the forms and literature to be provided in braille or audiotape on request. These are likely to be reasonable steps for the housing benefit office to have to take.

Provision for people with other disabilities or multiple disabilities

5.28 There are many examples of how auxiliary aids or services can be used to improve communication with people who have hearing disabilities or visual impairments. Service providers should also consider how communication barriers can be overcome for people with other disabilities. For example, a customer with a learning disability may be able to access a service by the provision of documents in large, clear print and plain language or by the use of colour coding and illustrations.

A coach company issues its staff at a ticket office with a card showing destinations, types of tickets and prices. It trains the staff so that customers with learning disabilities can point to or ask for the options on the card that they want. These are likely to be reasonable steps for the coach company to have to take.

5.29 Service providers should not assume that their services are made accessible to customers with multiple disabilities simply by providing auxiliary aids or services which are suitable for people with individual disabilities.

5.30 For example, deafblind people (individuals who have a severe combined sight and hearing impairment) are not necessarily assisted in accessing services by the simple provision of communication aids designed for use by people with hearing disabilities or visual impairments. Such aids could assist deafblind people if appropriately used (for example, information leaflets produced in braille or Moon, good lighting and acoustics, induction loop systems, etc). However, what is appropriate will depend on the nature and extent of the individual's dual sensory impairment and the methods he or she uses to communicate and access information. Adjustments which may be of assistance to a deafblind person might include engaging a deafblind manual interpreter for important meetings or having a member of staff trained in specific ways to help a deafblind person. Where service providers give their staff disability awareness training, they should consider including ways of helping deafblind people, such as guiding them safely and tracing capital letters and numbers on the palm of the hand.

A branch of a bank with a regular customer who is deafblind has a particular staff member trained in communicating with deafblind people. At the customer's request, the bank arranges for statements and letters to be sent in braille. These are likely to be reasonable steps for the bank to have to take.

Overcoming barriers created by physical features

What is the duty to make reasonable adjustments in relation to physical features?

5.31 Where a 'physical feature' makes it impossible or unreasonably difficult for disabled people to make use of any service which is offered to the public, a service provider must take reasonable steps to:

- remove the feature; or

- alter it so that it no longer has that effect; or

- provide a reasonable means of avoiding the feature; or

- provide a reasonable alternative method of making the service available to disabled people.

s 21(2)

The meaning of a 'physical feature' is explained in paragraph 5.44 below and includes, for example, a feature arising from the design or construction of a building or the approach or access to premises.

5.32 The duty to make reasonable adjustments in relation to a physical feature sets out four possible ways in which the barriers created by such features might be overcome. The fourth duty – to provide a reasonable alternative method of making the service available – has been in force since 1 October 1999. The other duties come into force on 1 October 2004.

5.33 Whilst service providers are not obliged to comply with these latter duties – to remove, alter or provide a reasonable means of avoiding a physical feature – prior to 1 October 2004, the Code of Practice has been issued in advance of this date to give service providers an opportunity to consider the adjustments that they need to make under these provisions. The period between the issue of this Code and 1 October 2004 is intended to be a 'transitional' period during which service providers can prepare for their new obligations. It will be good practice and may make business sense to take action to remove or alter a physical feature or to provide a reasonable means of avoiding it before October 2004 and there is nothing to prevent a service provider from doing so.

5.34 In considering whether or not a service provider has taken reasonable steps to comply with its duties after 1 October 2004, a court might take into account the time that the service provider has had prior to that date to make preparations.

A public inquiry point is located on the second floor of a government office building and is accessed by a flight of stairs. This makes it impossible or unreasonably difficult for some disabled people to get to it. People with a mobility disability or a mental health disability (like anxiety related depression) may find using the stairs difficult.

Since 1 October 1999 the government department has had to consider what it could do to provide a reasonable alternative method of making its inquiry service accessible to disabled members of the public. For example, it might provide the service in the form of a telephone inquiry line. This may be a reasonable alternative method of providing the service if it effectively delivers the service in another way.

However, if it does not do so (for instance, if staff at the inquiry point also help people to complete forms and that cannot be done by telephone), the provision of a telephone service may not be a reasonable alternative. The department will then have to consider whether there are other reasonable steps it can take to provide the same service. For example, it might provide a courtesy telephone on the ground floor to enable disabled people to call staff down to help them.

Despite this, if the service is still not accessible to all disabled people, from 1 October 2004 further reasonable steps may involve a physical alteration of some kind. For example, it might be reasonable to install a lift or to move the inquiry point to the ground floor. Although there is no requirement to make physical alterations before 1 October 2004, it may be sensible to consider and give effect to such possibilities before then, especially if refurbishment of the building is being planned.

5.35 It would be sensible for service providers to plan ahead and to apply for any necessary consents before 1 October 2004 so they are able to make any physical alterations. Whenever a service provider is planning and executing building or refurbishment works, such as extending existing premises or making structural alterations to an existing building, it is sensible to provide for the removal or alteration of physical features which create a barrier to access for disabled people or to consider providing a reasonable means of avoiding the physical feature. Even though the Act does not require this until 1 October 2004, it might be more cost effective to make these alterations as part of planned refurbishment before 2004.

A public launderette is planning to install new washing machines and tumble dryers in 2002. In doing so, it chooses the machines and their positioning so as to facilitate their use by disabled customers. This has the effect of improving the accessibility of the launderette to disabled people.

A firm of accountants is refurbishing its offices in 2001. In replacing the carpets, the firm ensures that low pile, high density carpeting is fitted. This helps many of its clients with mobility impairments (for example, those who use a wheelchair, artificial limb or walking aid) to move with greater ease within the office. The firm also decides to make improvements to the office lighting and signage. This aids its clients with visual, hearing or learning disabilities. As part of the refurbishment, the firm also fits braille markings to lift buttons and installs an induction loop system in one of its meeting rooms. By these means, the firm has placed itself in a good position to provide accessible services to its disabled clients.

What are a service provider's obligations in respect of physical features?

5.36 The Act does not require a service provider to adopt one way of meeting its obligations rather than another. The focus of the Act is on results. Where there is a physical barrier, the service provider's aim should be to make its services accessible to disabled people. What is important is that this aim is achieved, rather than how it is achieved. If a service remains inaccessible, a service provider may have to defend its decisions.

**s 19(1)(b),
s 21(2)**

5.37 For example, a service provider may decide to provide a service by the option of an alternative method. If the result is that disabled people are then able to access the service without unreasonable difficulty, that will satisfy the service provider's obligations under the Act. If, on the other hand, it is still unreasonably difficult for a disabled person to make use of the service, the service provider would then have to show that it could not have reasonably removed or altered the physical feature, or provided a reasonable means of avoiding it. The cost of taking such action may be a relevant consideration. Similarly, if the service provider takes no action, it will have to show that there were no steps which it could reasonably have taken. The kinds of factors which may be relevant in deciding what are reasonable steps for a service provider to have to take are described in paragraphs 4.21 to 4.27 above.

An estate agent is marketing a new residential property development. It decides to hold detailed presentations for prospective buyers at the company's premises, at which there will be a talk illustrated with slides. However, the only meeting room available in the building is inaccessible to many disabled people. The estate agent obtains a quotation to make its premises more accessible, but the cost is more than it anticipated, and it delays making the alterations.

When disabled people who are unable to attend a presentation because the room is inaccessible to them make enquiries, they are merely sent copies of comparatively brief promotional literature. This is unlikely to be a reasonable alternative method of making the service available.

If an issue arose under the Act as to whether the estate agent had failed to comply with its obligations to disabled people who are unable to make use of its service, regard might be had to the reasonableness of making the service available by any of the four different ways set out in the Act for complying with the duty to make reasonable adjustments in relation to barriers created by physical features. In this case, this would involve consideration of whether it would have been reasonable to avoid the feature, such as by holding the meeting at another venue, whether there was a more effective alternative method of providing the service that could reasonably have been adopted, or whether the cost the company would have incurred in altering its premises was such that this would have been a reasonable step for it to have to take.

Adopting an 'inclusive' approach

5.38 It is in the interests of both service providers and disabled people to overcome physical features that prevent or limit disabled people from using the services that are offered. Although the Act does not place the different options for overcoming a physical feature in any form of hierarchy, it is recognised good practice for a service provider to consider first whether a physical feature which creates a barrier for disabled people can be removed or altered.

5.39 This is because removing or altering the barriers created by a physical feature is an 'inclusive' approach to adjustments. It makes the services available to everyone in the same way. In contrast, an alternative method of service offers disabled people a different form of service than is provided for non-disabled people.

5.40 Removing or altering the barriers created by a physical feature will also be preferable to any alternative arrangements from the standpoint of the dignity of disabled people. In addition, it is likely to be in the long-term interests of the service provider, since it will avoid the ongoing costs of providing services by alternative means and may expand the customer base.

5.41 Therefore, it is recommended that service providers should first consider whether any physical features which create a barrier for disabled people can be removed or altered. If that is not reasonable, a service provider should then consider providing a reasonable means of avoiding the physical feature. If that is also not reasonable, the service provider should then consider providing a reasonable alternative method of making the service available to disabled people.

How can service providers identify possible adjustments?

5.42 Service providers are more likely to be able to comply with their duty to make adjustments in relation to physical features if they arrange for an access audit of their premises to be conducted and draw up an access plan or strategy. Acting on the results of such an evaluation may reduce the likelihood of legal claims against the service provider.

5.43 In carrying out an audit, it is recommended that service providers seek the views of people with different disabilities, or those representing them, to assist in identifying barriers and developing effective solutions. Service providers can also draw on the extensive experience of local and national disability groups or organisations of disabled people.

What is a 'physical feature'?

s 21(2)
SI 1999/1191
regs 2-3

5.44 The *Disability Discrimination (Services and Premises)* Regulations 1999 make provision for various things to be treated as physical features. A 'physical feature' includes:

■ any feature arising from the design or construction of a building on the premises occupied by the service provider;

■ any feature on those premises or any approach to, exit from or access to such a building;

■ any fixtures, fittings, furnishings, furniture, equipment or materials in or on such premises;

■ any fixtures, fittings, furnishings, furniture, equipment or materials brought onto premises (other than those occupied by the service provider) by or on behalf of the service provider in the course of (and for the purpose of) providing services to the public;

■ any other physical element or quality of land comprised in the premises occupied by the service provider.

All these features are covered whether temporary or permanent. A building means an erection or structure of any kind.

5.45 Physical features will include steps, stairways, kerbs, exterior surfaces and paving, parking areas, building entrances and exits (including emergency escape routes), internal and external doors, gates, toilet and washing facilities, public facilities (such as telephones, counters or service desks), lighting and ventilation, lifts and escalators, floor coverings, signs, furniture, and temporary or movable items (such as equipment and display racks). This is not an exhaustive list.

5.46 Where physical features are within the boundaries of a service provider's premises and are making it impossible or unreasonably difficult for disabled people to use the service, then the duty to make reasonable adjustments will apply. This will be the case even if the physical features are outdoors; for example, the paths and seating in a pub garden.

5.47 Where the physical features are within the remit of a highway authority and the highway authority is a service provider, it will have a duty to make reasonable adjustments.

A highway authority has placed some benches on the pavement of a busy main road which is also a shopping street. These benches are very low and have no arms. Some disabled people are finding them very difficult to use. The highway authority decides to make simple alterations to the benches so that they have arms and are slightly higher. This is likely to be a reasonable step for the authority to have to take.

Removing the physical feature

5.48 Removing the physical feature may be a reasonable step – and the most effective one – for a service provider to take. Physical features often create physical barriers which impede disabled people accessing services.

Display units at the entrance of a small shop restrict the ability of wheelchair users to enter the shop. The owner decides that, without any significant loss of selling space, the display units can be removed and repositioned elsewhere in the shop. This is likely to be a reasonable step for the shop to have to take.

A countryside visitor centre includes, as an attraction, a lakeside walk. However, a stile prevents access to the lakeside walk for those with mobility difficulties. The park authority which runs the centre removes the stile and replaces it with an accessible gate. This is likely to be a reasonable step for the service provider to have to take.

Altering the physical feature

5.49 Altering the physical feature so that it no longer has the effect of making it impossible or unreasonably difficult for disabled people to use the services may also be a reasonable step for a service provider to take.

A local religious group holds prayer meetings in a building entered by steps. The room in which the prayer meetings are held has a narrow entrance door. To ensure that its prayer meetings are accessible to disabled people, the religious group installs a permanent ramp at the entrance to the building. It also widens the door to the room. These are likely to be reasonable steps for the religious group to have to take.

Providing a reasonable means of avoiding the physical feature

5.50 Providing a reasonable means of avoiding the physical feature may also be a reasonable step for a service provider to take.

A public art gallery is accessible by a flight of stairs at its front entrance. It is housed in a listed building, and has not been able to obtain consent to install a ramped entrance to the gallery. A side entrance for staff use is fully accessible and always open. The gallery arranges for people with a mobility impairment to use this entrance. This is likely to be a reasonable step for the gallery to have to take. It could of course go further and adopt an inclusive approach by also making the side entrance available to everyone.

5.51 The Act requires that any means of avoiding the physical feature must be a 'reasonable' one. Relevant considerations in this respect may include whether the provision of the service in this way significantly offends the dignity of disabled people and the extent to which it causes disabled people inconvenience.

A firm of solicitors is located in a building whose front entrance is only accessible by climbing a flight of stairs. At ground level there is a bell and a sign saying 'Please ring for disabled access.' However, the bell is not answered promptly, even in bad weather, so that a disabled person often has to wait for an unreasonable time before gaining access to the building. This is unlikely to be a reasonable means of avoiding thefeature.

Providing a reasonable alternative method of making services available

5.52 Providing a reasonable alternative method of making services available to disabled people may also be a reasonable step for a service provider to take. The Act requires that any alternative method of making services available must be a 'reasonable' one. Relevant considerations in this respect may include whether the provision of the service in this way significantly offends the dignity of disabled people and the extent to which it causes disabled people inconvenience.

A small self-service pharmacist's shop has goods displayed on high shelving separated by narrow aisles. It is not practicable to alter this arrangement. The goods are not easily accessible to many disabled people. The shop decides to provide a customer assistance service. On request, a member of staff locates goods and brings them to the cash till for a disabled customer. This is the provision of a service by an alternative method, which makes the service accessible for disabled people. This is likely to be a reasonable step for the shop to have to take.

The changing facilities in a women-only gym are located in a room which is only accessible by stairs. The service provider suggests to disabled users of the gym with mobility impairments that they can change in a corner of the gym itself. This is unlikely to be a reasonable alternative method of making the service available, since it may significantly infringe their dignity.

How do building regulations and leases affect reasonable adjustments?

Introduction

6.1 In **Chapters 4** and **5** of the Code, an explanation is given of the duty to make reasonable adjustments and how it works in practice, including the duties that will apply from 1 October 2004 in respect of overcoming physical barriers. This chapter addresses the issues of how building regulations and leases affect the duty to make reasonable adjustments to physical features where they make it impossible or unreasonably difficult for disabled people to use a service.

Building regulations

Summary

6.2 A building in England or Wales that complies with Part M of Building Regulations (see paragraph 6.4 below) should make reasonable provision for disabled people to gain access to and use the building. Broadly, a building will comply with Part M when its physical features (or aspects of physical features) accord with those described in the Approved Document M (see paragraph 6.6 below). These will make it 'reasonably safe and convenient' for disabled people to gain access to and within a building and to use it. As the paragraphs below explain, an exemption set out in Regulations (see paragraph 6.7 below) means that a service provider who provides services from a building will not have to make alterations or adjustments

Approved Document M

ISBN 0 11 752447 6

ISBN 011 753469 2

to physical features which accord with Approved Document M if 10 years or less have passed since their construction or installation.

6.3 The Approved Document M is not mandatory, however, and it is open to a developer to comply with Part M in other ways. Only certain features are addressed in the Approved Document. Where a building complies with Part M any alternative treatment of those features must enable any disabled person to use the building with the same degree of ease as would have been the case had those features (or aspects of those features) accorded with those set out in the Approved Document. Therefore a service provider who provides services from such a building is unlikely to have to make alterations or adjustments to those specific features if 10 years or less have passed since their construction or installation (see paragraph 6.8 below). The position is similar in Scotland.

Requirements

SI 2000/2531

6.4 Since 1985 building regulations in England and Wales have required reasonable provisions to be made for disabled people to gain access to and to use new buildings (and some extensions). Part M of the Building Regulations (Access and facilities for disabled people), was extended in 1992 and again in 1999. It now applies to:

■ New buildings, and

■ Ground floor extensions to existing buildings but not the existing buildings themselves.

Buildings to which Part M applies should make reasonable provision for access and use by disabled people.

6.5 Where an extension has its own entrance it is treated as a new building but where it is accessed through the existing building the extension need not be any more accessible than the existing building. When alterations or extensions are made they should not have the effect of reducing the level of access to the existing building.

6.6 Guidance is issued to accompany the building regulations. For Part M of the Building Regulations in England and Wales this is the Approved Document M. This sets out a number of 'objectives' to be met, 'design considerations' and technical details of design solutions (called 'provisions'). These provisions suggest one way in which the requirements of the regulations might be met but there is no obligation to adopt any of them. Most buildings will have followed the guidance in the Approved Document, but some will have adopted other acceptable design solutions.

ISBN 011 752447 6

ISBN 0 11 753469 2

6.7 Some disabled people might find it impossible or unreasonably difficult to use services provided at a building even though the building meets the requirements of Part M. In this situation, if a physical feature accords with the 1992 or 1999 Approved Documents to Part M, an exemption provided by The Disability Discrimination (Providers of Services) (Adjustment of Premises) Regulations 2001 (the '2001 Regulations') means that the service provider will not have to make adjustments to that feature if 10 years or less have passed since it was constructed or installed. This is explained in paragraphs 6.12 below.

SI 2001/3253 reg 3(3)

6.8 A building with features which do not accord with the effective edition of the Approved Document (see paragraph 6.12 below) may have been accepted as meeting the requirements of Part M. If the feature is one which is covered by the Approved Document (for example, a lift) then, provided it enables any disabled person to access and use the building with the same degree of ease as would have been the case had the feature accorded with the Approved Document, it is unlikely to be reasonable for a service provider to have to make adjustments to that feature if 10 years or less have passed since its installation or construction. This is because the 2001 Regulations are not intended to deter people from adopting effective innovative or alternative design. Where a feature is one which is not covered by the Approved Document (for example, lighting) then under the DDA the service provider may still have to make adjustments to that feature.

A sports centre built in 1995 in England has a shower compartment for use by disabled customers. The centre was subject to scrutiny by a Building Control Officer. In his opinion the design provided reasonable access for disabled people, sufficient to satisfy Part M of the Building Regulations. The shower compartment has a seat fixed to the floor rather than a tip up seat as shown in Approved Document M because the partition walls will not bear the weight of a tip up seat. The fixed seat means it is difficult for some disabled people to use the shower. It would nonetheless be unlikely to be reasonable for the sports centre to have to consider changing the seating arrangements in the shower cubicle until 2005.

6.9   Similar provisions to those in England and Wales were also introduced in Scotland in 1985 when 'facilities for disabled persons' were added to the Building Standards (Scotland) Regulations. As in England and Wales, there have been various versions. From April 1991 until April 2000 the detailed requirements for compliance with the Building Standards (Scotland) Regulations 1990 were set out in Part T of the Technical Standards. In April 2000 Part T was discontinued and its requirements were integrated into the general Technical Standards.

6.10   In Scotland the Technical Standards apply to:

- New buildings,

- Conversions,

- Extensions to existing buildings but not the existing buildings themselves,

- Parts of a building that are altered or that are adversely affected by an alteration being carried out elsewhere in the building, and

- Parts of a building that are subject to a change of use.

6.11   The Technical Standards stipulate requirements that must be met in order to comply with the building standards regulations. In general, no building work of a type that is subject to the regulations may be carried out without a warrant from the Local Authority. The Local Authority will only grant a warrant if the building works proposed comply with the Technical Standards. However, a standard may be relaxed or dispensed with entirely if it is considered to be unreasonable in a particular situation. Where this occurs it is unlikely to be reasonable for a service provider to have to make adjustments to relevant physical features for a period of 10 years from their installation or construction (see paragraphs 6.2 to 6.3 above). An exemption from the duty to make reasonable

SI 2001/3253 reg 3 (3)

adjustments to physical features applies where those features accord with the relevant version of Part T or the corresponding requirements in the Technical Standards introduced in April 2000 and March 2002 (see paragraph 6.17 below).

Where the exemption applies in England and Wales

SI 2001/3253
Sch, para 2

6.12   The overall effect of the 2001 Regulations is that, for a period of 10 years, a service provider in England and Wales need not remove or alter any aspect of a physical feature of a building that accords with the relevant objectives, design considerations and provisions in the Approved Document M. At the date of publication of the Code, the effective edition of the Approved Document M will be either the1992 or 1999 edition. For building works where the building regulations applied, the effective edition will be the version which applied in meeting those building regulations. For building works where the building regulations did not apply the effective edition will be that which was in force when those works commenced. Any building works undertaken before I October 1994 will not be protected by the exemption.

6.13   The service provider may still however be required to provide:

■   a reasonable means of avoiding that feature; or

■   a reasonable alternative method of making services available.

6.14   In England and Wales there are areas of development, such as alterations, where Part M of the Building Regulations does not require that accessibility be improved. Despite the absence of any legal obligation under the building regulations, a service provider may still decide to adopt the guidance in the Approved Document M. Physical features that the service provider includes, that accord with the objectives, design considerations and provisions set out in the relevant Approved Document M, will not have to be removed or altered if 10 years or less have passed since their construction or installation.

A corner shop was converted to a social services neighbourhood office in 1996. A ramp was installed to the front door and all internal doors were widened. The length and gradient of the ramp accord with the provisions set out in the applicable Approved Document M (1992) and the doors provide the recommended clear opening width. The service provider would not be required under Part III of the DDA to alter the length or gradient of the ramp or the internal door widths before 2006.

6.15 The 10 year exemption period commences from the date the installation of that feature was completed or, where the physical feature is installed as part of a larger building project, from the date the works in relation to that project were completed. The 2001 Regulations do not stipulate how the date will be established. However, it is likely that in the majority of cases it will be the day on which the service provider is able to make use of the physical feature. Where industry standard forms of contract are used this is known as 'practical completion' and is the date on which the contractor hands over the work to the service provider.

**SI 2001/3253
Sch, para 1(3)**

The toilets in a restaurant were redecorated in 1996. The service provider took the opportunity to install handrails in one of the cubicles, in accordance with the provisions of the applicable Approved Document M (1992), to assist people with ambulant disabilities. The service provider finished the work and the toilets were brought back into use on 15 June 1996. The service provider would be exempted from any requirement under Part III to replace or alter those handrails before 15 June 2006, when the exemption elapses.

The construction of a large department store in England began in 1997 and practical completion was achieved on 27 July 1999. The width of the main entrance and the dimensions of the lobby accord with those set out in the provisions of the applicable Approved Document M (1992). The service provider would be exempted from any requirement under Part III to replace or alter the width of the door or the size of the lobby before 27 July 2009, when the exemption elapses.

6.16   If new guidance is brought into effect to replace the 1999 editionof the Approved Document M, new DDA regulations might provide a similar exemption. Service providers whose premises include physical features that are constructed in accordance with the revised design guidance should check whether the 2001 Regulations have been amended before relying on them to justify a decision not to remove or alter any of those features.

Where the exemption applies in Scotland

6.17 The 2001 Regulations make similar provisions in Scotland but take into account the fact that in Scotland the requirements to provide access and facilities for disabled people are now dispersed among the general Technical Standards (see paragraph 6.9 above). However, the general effect of the 2001 Regulations is the same. That is, for a period of 10 years, a service provider need not remove or alter any aspect of a physical feature of a building that accords with the relevant version of Part T or the corresponding requirements now included in other Technical Standards introduced in April 2000 and March 2002.

SI 2001/3253 reg 3(3)

SI 1994/1266; SI 1996/2251; SI 1997/2157; SSI 1999/173; SSI 2001/320

6.18 The relevant standard will be that which was in effect at the time the works to install the physical feature commenced, provided they did not commence before 30 June 1994 or after the Technical Standards 2001 (commencing as of 3 March 2002) cease to have effect. Where an application for a warrant for the construction or change of use of the building has been made and granted, the works are deemed to commence on the day the application for the warrant was made.

SI 2001/3253 Sch, para 1 (2),(3)

6.19 The service provider may still however be required to provide:

■ a reasonable means of avoiding that feature; or

■ a reasonable alternative method of making services available.

6.20 The 10 year exemption period commences from the date the installation of that feature was completed or, where the physical feature is installed as part of a larger building project,

SI 2001/3253 Sch, para 1(3)

97

from the date the works in relation to that project were completed. The 2001 Regulations do not stipulate how the date will be established. However, it is likely that in the majority of cases it will be the day on which the service provider is able to make use of the physical feature.

> The construction of a health centre in Scotland was completed in 1998 in accordance with the applicable version of Part T. The health authority, as the service provider in these circumstances, is not exempt from the duty to remove or alter any physical feature of the building beyond 2008 when the 10 year period elapses.

6.21 If new Technical Standards are brought into effect new DDA regulations might provide a similar exemption. Service providers whose premises are constructed in accordance with future Technical Standards should check whether the 2001 Regulations have been amended before relying on them to justify a decision not to remove or alter any of those features.

Application of the exemption throughout Great Britain

6.22 The exemption relates only to the particular aspect of the physical feature in question, that accords with the provisions of the Approved Document M in England and Wales or the relevant Technical Standard in Scotland and not to the building as a whole.

The dimensions of the risers and treads of steps to the entrance of a multi screen cinema (built in 1996) accord with the provisions of the relevant Approved Document M (1992). Those aspects of the steps will not have to be altered for a period of 10 years from the date their installation was complete. That is not to say that the service provider will not have to improve access to its premises in other ways and it may still have to consider improving the accessibility of the steps by, for instance, improving the lighting or fitting a non-slip surface treatment.

6.23 Where a particular aspect of a physical feature accorded with the applicable provision in the relevant Approved Document M, or Technical Standard in Scotland, no alteration will be required, so long as it continues to accord with the provision. The exemption will last for 10 years from the date that the feature was constructed or installed. It will not apply to other aspects of the same feature if they did not conform with or were not covered by the provisions in the guidance.

The clear opening width of the door to a restaurant (built in Wales in 1998) conformed to the relevant provision of the Approved Document M. The service provider would not be expected to consider altering the width of the door, under Part III of the DDA, until 2008. If, however, in 2002 the door was replaced by a narrower one, which no longer provided the clear opening width described in the provisions of the Approved Document M, then this aspect of the feature would no longer be exempt from a possible requirement for alteration.

In any event, the service provider might have to consider altering other aspects of the door's design (for example, the type of handle, the colour or the weight of the door) that are not covered by the Approved Document M.

6.24 Service providers should be aware of the limited scope of the Approved Document M or Technical Standards in Scotland. For those aspects of design that fall beyond their scope, service providers are recommended to take account of the wealth of published advice on the principles and practice of 'inclusive design'. For instance, building regulations do not cover the design of the external environment (except for those features that are needed to provide access to the building from the edge of the site and from car parking within the site) nor does it cover the provision of signage.

The design of a new visitors' centre in a Welsh country park adopts in full the guidance provided in the Approved Document M. Once the centre is open to the public the manager receives a number of complaints from people with mobility and visual impairments who find that stiles and gates along the centre's nature trail are extremely difficult to negotiate. There is no guidance on the design of these physical features in the Approved Document M. Consequently they would not be exempt from a possible requirement for alteration under Part III of the DDA.

There is no signage to assist people with visual impairments within the visitors' centre with the result that some people become disorientated and are unable to locate the toilets or cafeteria. The service provider would be expected to consider what reasonable steps might be taken to remedy the situation, including the provision of signage.

6.25   The Approved Document M in England and Wales and the Technical Standards in Scotland describe circumstances where the requirement might be met despite the fact that certain physical features, which would facilitate access, are not provided on the premises. The exemption only applies to a physical feature that was included (and which accords with the provisions of the relevant Approved Document M or Technical Standard). It does not apply to a physical feature that was not required and therefore not included on the premises. The service provider will need to consider whether the provision of those features would be reasonable under Part III of the DDA.

The designer of a library built in Scotland in 1997 was careful to adopt all relevant provisions of Part T of the Technical Standards. A deaf person who uses a hearing aid cannot participate fully in seminars convened in the small meeting room because there is no induction loop in it. The exemption does not apply even though the Technical Standard states that induction loops need not be provided in meeting rooms of this size. The service provider would have to consider whether it would be reasonable under Part III of the DDA to provide an induction loop in this room.

Leases, binding obligations and reasonable adjustments

6.26 Set out in paragraphs 6.27 to 6.49 below are those issues which are relevant to service providers who occupy premises under a lease, or other binding obligation, in terms of their duty to make reasonable adjustments, particularly in relation to removing or altering physical barriers. These include arrangements for obtaining consent for alterations.

6.27 Service providers should remember that even where consent is not given for removing or altering a physical feature, they still have a duty to consider providing a reasonable means of avoiding a feature or providing the service by a reasonable alternative means (see Chapter 5).

What about the need to obtain statutory consent for some building changes?

s 59

6.28 A service provider might have to obtain statutory consent before making adjustments involving changes to premises. Such consents include planning permission, building regulations approval or a building warrant in Scotland, listed building consent, scheduled monument consent and fire regulations approval. The Act does not override the need to obtain such consents.

6.29 Service providers should plan for and anticipate the need to obtain consent to make a particular adjustment. It might take time to obtain such consent, but it could be reasonable to make an interim or other adjustment – one that does not require consent – in the meantime.

A historic country house is open to the public. To enable visitors with a mobility impairment to visit the house, the owners are considering installing a ramped entrance. In the circumstances, installing a ramp is likely to be a reasonable adjustment for the service provider to have to make.

However, the service provider in this case needs statutory consent to do so because the house is a listed building. The service provider consults the local planning authority and learns that consent is likely to be given in a few weeks. In the meantime, as a temporary measure only, the service provider arranges for disabled visitors to use an inconvenient but accessible entrance at the side of the house. Although not ideal, this is likely to be an acceptable solution for a limited period while statutory consent is being obtained.

6.30 Where consent has been refused, there is likely to be a means of appeal. Whether or not the service provider's duty to take such steps as it is reasonable to take includes pursuing an appeal will depend on the circumstances of the case.

What if a binding obligation other than a lease prevents a building being altered?

6.31 The service provider may be bound by the terms of an agreement or other legally binding obligation (for example, a mortgage, charge or restrictive covenant or, in Scotland, a feu disposition) under which he cannot alter the premises without someone else's consent. In these circumstances, the 2001 Regulations provide that it is reasonable for the service provider to have to request that consent, but

SI 2001/3253 reg 3(2)

that it is not reasonable for the service provider to have to make an alteration before having obtained that consent.

> A church holds social functions in the church hall, built with the assistance of a bank loan. The bank loan is secured by way of a charge on the hall under which the bank's consent is required for any changes. The church is proposing to make alterations to the hall to comply with its duty to make reasonable adjustments. It is reasonable for the church to have to seek the bank's consent but it is not reasonable for the church to have to make the alteration if the bank does not give its consent.

What happens if a lease says that certain changes to premises cannot be made?

s 27 (2)

6.32 Special provisions apply where a service provider occupies premises under a lease, the terms of which prevent it from making an alteration to the premises. In such circumstances, if the alteration is one which the service provider proposes to make in order to comply with a duty of reasonable adjustment, the Act overrides the terms of the lease so as to entitle the service provider to make the alteration with the consent of its landlord ('the lessor'). In such a case the service provider must first write to the lessor asking for consent to make the alteration. The lessor cannot unreasonably withhold consent but may attach reasonable conditions to the consent.

6.33 If the service provider fails to make a written application to the lessor for consent to the alteration, the service provider will not be able to rely upon the fact that the lease has a term preventing it from making alterations to the premises to defend its failure to make an alteration. In these circumstances, anything in the lease which prevents that alteration being made must be ignored in deciding whether it was reasonable for the service provider to have made the alteration.

Sch 4, Part II para 5

> A service provider occupies premises under a lease, a term of which says that the service provider cannot make alterations to a staircase. When deciding whether or not it was reasonable for the service provider to make an alteration to the staircase in order to make it more accessible to disabled people, a court will ignore the terms of the lease unless the service provider has written to ask the lessor for permission to make the alteration.

What happens if the lessor has a 'superior' lessor?

6.34 The service provider's lessor may himself hold a lease the terms of which prevent him from consenting to the alteration without the consent of his landlord ('the superior lessor'). The 2001 Regulations made under the Act cover this by modifying the effect of any superior lease so as to require the lessee of that lease to apply in writing to his lessor (the 'superior lessor' in this context) if he wishes to consent to the alteration. As with the service provider's lessor, the superior lessor must not withhold such consent unreasonably but may attach reasonable conditions to the lease.

SI 2001/3253 reg 9

> A bakery occupies the premises under a lease, the terms of which prevent it from making alterations without the consent of its landlord. The landlord holds the premises under a lease which has a similar term. The landlord receives an application from the bakery for consent to alter the premises. He is entitled to consent to the application if he receives the consent of his landlord. He writes to his landlord asking for that consent. His landlord cannot unreasonably refuse to give consent but may consent subject to reasonable conditions.

6.35 Where a superior lessor receives an application from his lessee the provisions described in paragraphs 6.36 to 6.49 below apply as if his lessee were the service provider.

How will arrangements for gaining consent work?

reg 5(2),(6)

6.36 Once the application has been made, as a general rule the lessor has 42 days, beginning with the day on which he receives the application, to reply in writing to the service provider (or the person who made the application on its behalf). If he fails to do so he is taken to have withheld his consent to the alteration and the provisions described in paragraph 6.47 below apply.

reg 5(3),(4)

6.37 However, the lessor has 21 days to make a written request for any plans and specifications that it is reasonable for him to require and which were not included with the application. If he makes such a request the 42 day period will begin with the day on which he receives the plans and specifications. It would be sensible, in order to ensure that the application is dealt with as speedily as possible, for service providers to include the plans and specifications with the application for consent.

6.38 If the lessor replies consenting to the application subject to obtaining the consent of another person (required under a superior lease or because of a binding obligation), but he fails to seek the consent of the other person within 42 days of receiving the application (or receiving the plans and specifications, if these arrive later), he will be taken to have withheld his consent and the provisions described in paragraph 6.47 below apply.

reg 5(2),(4)

6.39 The 2001 Regulations provide that a lessor will be treated as not having sought the consent of another person unless:

reg 5(7)

- the lessor has applied in writing to the other person indicating that the occupier has asked for consent for an alteration in order to comply with a duty to make reasonable adjustments, and the lessor has given his consent conditionally upon obtaining the other person's consent; and

- he has submitted to the other person any plans and specifications which he has received.

6.40 A lessor who receives the consent required from another person will also be taken to have withheld his consent if he fails within 14 days to let the service provider (or the person who made the application on behalf of the service provider) know in writing that he has received consent.

reg 5(5)

A gift shop wishes to alter its entrance to make it more accessible. It applies to the lessor for consent to make the alteration and encloses plans and specifications with the application. The lessor is content for the alteration to be made but he has mortgaged the premises with a bank. The terms of the mortgage require him to obtain the bank's consent before making or permitting any alteration.

Within 42 days of receiving the application the lessor writes to the shop saying that he will consent to the alteration if the bank agrees. At the same time he applies in writing to the bank for consent. He encloses the plans and specifications with the application and makes clear that the shop wishes to make the alteration to comply with the reasonable adjustments duty. He also makes clear to the bank that he has consented to the alteration, provided the bank gives its consent. The bank replies to the lessor, giving its consent and the lessor informs the shop of this within 14 days of receiving the consent.

When is it unreasonable for a lessor to withhold consent?

6.41 Whether withholding consent will be reasonable or not will depend on the specific circumstances. For example, if a particular adjustment is likely to result in a substantial permanent reduction in the value of the lessor's interest in the premises, the lessor is likely to be acting reasonably in withholding consent. The lessor is also likely to be acting reasonably if he withholds consent because an adjustment would cause significant disruption or inconvenience to other tenants (for example, where the premises consist of multiple adjoining units).

6.42 A trivial or arbitrary reason would almost certainly be unreasonable. Many reasonable adjustments to premises will not harm the lessor's interests and so it would generally be unreasonable to withhold consent for them.

A florist occupies shop premises in a row of shops which are part of a new marina complex. The shop is leased from the marina owner. To comply with its duties under the Act, the florist wishes to improve the accessibility of the shop to disabled people by the provision of a wider front door. It seeks permission to do so from the marina owner who refuses permission on the ground that all the shops in the marina must have the same appearance. It is likely to be unreasonable to withhold consent in these circumstances.

6.43 The 2001 Regulations provide that it is unreasonable for a lessor to withhold consent in circumstances where the lease says that consent will be given to alterations of the kind for which consent has been sought.

reg 6

6.44 The 2001 Regulations provide that withholding consent will be reasonable where:

reg 7

- there is a binding obligation requiring the consent of any person to the alteration;

- the lessor has taken steps to seek consent; and

- consent has not been given or has been given subject to a condition making it reasonable for the lessor to withhold his consent.

Withholding consent will also be reasonable where a lessor does not know, and could not reasonably be expected to know, that the alteration is a reasonable adjustment.

In the example in paragraph 6.42 above, the original developer of the marina sold it to the present owner (the lessor of the florist shop) with an enforceable restrictive covenant requiring the developer's consent to any alteration to the façade or appearance of the marina shops. The lessor has applied for that consent, but it has been refused. In these circumstances, it will be reasonable for the lessor to refuse permission to the florist to make the alterations requested.

What conditions would it be reasonable for a lessor to make when giving consent?

6.45 The 2001 Regulations set out some conditions which it is reasonable for a lessor to make. Depending on the circumstances of the case there may be other conditions which it would be reasonable for a lessor to require the service provider to meet. Where a lessor imposes other conditions (for example, a reinstatement condition) their reasonableness may be challenged in the courts (see paragraph 6.47 below).

reg 8   6.46 The conditions set out in the Regulations as ones which a lessor may reasonably require a service provider to meet are that it:

- obtains any necessary planning permission and other statutory consents;

- carries out the work in accordance with any plans and specifications approved by the lessor;

- allows the lessor a reasonable opportunity to inspect the work (whether before or after it is completed);

- reimburses the lessor's reasonable costs incurred in connection with the giving of consent; or

- obtains the consent of another person required under a binding obligation or superior lease.

What happens if the lessor refuses consent or attaches conditions to consent?

Reference to Court

6.47 If the service provider has written to the lessor for consent to make an alteration and the lessor has refused consent or has attached conditions to his consent, the service provider or a disabled person who has an interest in the proposed alteration may refer the matter to a county court or, in Scotland, the sheriff court. The court will decide whether the lessor's refusal or any of the conditions are unreasonable. If it decides that they are, it may make an appropriate declaration or authorise the service provider to make the alteration under a court order (which may impose conditions on the service provider). Where the service provider occupies premises under a sub-lease or sub-tenancy, these provisions are modified to apply also to the service provider's landlord.

Sch 4, Part II, para 6

SI 2001/3253 reg 9(5), (6)

Joining lessors in proceedings

6.48 In any legal proceedings on a claim under Part III of the Act, involving a failure to make an alteration to premises, the disabled person concerned or the service provider may ask the court to direct that the lessor be made a party to

Sch 4, Part II, para 7

the proceedings. The court will grant that request if it is made before the hearing of the claim begins (unless it appears to the court that a different lessor should be made a party to the proceedings). It may refuse the request if it is made after the hearing of the claim begins. The request will not be granted if it is made after the court has determined the claim.

6.49   Where the lessor has been made a party to the proceedings, the court may determine whether the lessor has unreasonably refused consent to the alteration or has consented subject to unreasonable conditions. In either case, the court can:

■   make an appropriate declaration;

■   make an order authorising the service provider to make a specified alteration,

■   order the lessor to pay compensation to the disabled person.

The court may require the service provider to comply with any conditions specified in the order. If the court orders the lessor to pay compensation, it cannot also order the service provider to do so.

7

Can a service provider justify less favourable treatment or failure to make reasonable adjustments?

Introduction

7.1 A service provider should not be looking for reasons or excuses to discriminate against disabled people who wish to use its services. It is in the service provider's own best interests to ensure that its services are fully accessible to all customers.

7.2 However, in limited circumstances, the Act does permit a service provider to justify the less favourable treatment of a disabled person or a failure to make a reasonable adjustment. This cannot be used as a reason for a general exclusion of disabled people from access to services. The circumstances in which such treatment or failure might be justified are examined in this chapter.

7.3 There are special rules affecting the provision of insurance, guarantees and deposits (these are dealt with in **Chapter 8** below).

Less favourable treatment

7.4 A service provider discriminates against a disabled person if:

- for a reason which relates to the disabled person's disability, it treats him or her less favourably than it treats or would treat others to whom that reason does not or would not apply; **and**

s 20(1)(a)

- it cannot show that the treatment in question is **justified**.

Failure to make reasonable adjustments

7.5 A service provider also discriminates against a disabled person if:

- it fails to comply with a duty to make reasonable adjustments imposed on it under the Act in relation to the disabled person; **and**

- it cannot show that the failure to comply with that duty is justified.

7.6 Treating a disabled person less favourably for a reason related to disability or failing to comply with a duty to make reasonable adjustments may be justified only if:

- the service provider believes that one or more of the relevant conditions detailed in paragraphs 7.11 to 7.24 below are satisfied; **and**

- it is reasonable in all the circumstances of the case for that person to hold that opinion.

7.7 The conditions specified in the Act relate to:

- health or safety;
- the disabled person being incapable of entering into a contract;
- the service provider being otherwise unable to provide the service to the public;
- enabling the service provider to provide the service to the disabled person or other members of the public;
- the greater cost of providing a tailor-made service.

These are explained in more detail in paragraphs 7.11 to 7.25 below.

If the reason for less favourable treatment or failure to comply with a duty to make reasonable adjustments does not fall within one of the relevant conditions, it cannot be justified and will therefore be unlawful.

The general approach to justification

7.8 The test of justification is twofold; what did the service provider believe? (a subjective test) and was that belief reasonably held? (an objective test). A service provider does not have to be an expert on disability, but it should take into account all the circumstances, including any information which is available, any advice which it would be reasonable to seek, and the opinion of the disabled person. The service provider should also consider whether it could make reasonable adjustments so that there would no longer be any less favourable treatment to justify; for example, by amending an evacuation procedure where a refusal of service might otherwise be justified on health and safety grounds. The lawfulness of what a service provider does or fails to do will be judged by what it knew (or could reasonably have known), what it did and why it did it at the time of the alleged discriminatory act.

7.9 In some instances, it will not be clear whether any of the justifications apply. It may be shown subsequently that a service provider was mistaken in its opinion in a particular case. Coming to an incorrect conclusion does not necessarily mean that the service provider has discriminated unlawfully against a disabled person. In such cases, a service provider may be able to justify less favourable treatment or a failure to make reasonable adjustments if it can show that it was reasonable, in all the circumstances of the case, for it to hold that opinion at the time.

7.10   If a disabled person can show that he or she has been treated less favourably than others for a reason related to his or her disability, it is for the service provider to show that the action taken was justified. Similarly, if a disabled person can show that the service provider has failed to comply with a duty to make reasonable adjustments in relation to the disabled person, it is for the service provider to show that the failure was justified. In either case, the justification must fall within one of the relevant categories of justification set out in the Act and which are described in paragraphs 7.11 to 7.25 immediately below. Some of the categories of justification only apply to particular acts of otherwise unlawful discrimination.

Health or safety

s 20(4)(a)
s 20(9)

7.11   The Act does not require a service provider to do anything which would endanger the health or safety of any person. A service provider can justify less favourable treatment or a failure to make an adjustment if it is necessary in order not to endanger the health or safety of any person, including the disabled person in question.

An amusement park operator refuses to allow a person with muscular dystrophy onto a physically demanding, high speed ride. Because of her disability, the disabled person uses walking sticks and cannot stand unaided. The ride requires users to brace themselves using their legs. The refusal is based on genuine concerns for the health or safety of the disabled person and other users of the ride. This is likely to be justified.

7.12 The justification cannot apply unless the service provider reasonably believes that the treatment is necessary in order not to endanger the health or safety of any person. Health or safety reasons which are based on generalisations and stereotyping of disabled people provide no defence. For example, fire regulations should not be used as an excuse to place unnecessary restrictions on wheelchair users based on the assumption that wheelchair users would be an automatic hazard in a fire. It is for the management of the establishment concerned, with advice from the licensing authority or local fire officer, to make any special provision needed. Service providers should ensure that any action taken in relation to health or safety is proportionate to the risk. There must be a balance between protecting against the risk and restricting disabled people from using the service. Disabled people are entitled to make the same choices and to take the same risks within the same limits as other people.

Although there are adequate means of escape, a cinema manager turns away a wheelchair user because she assumes, without checking, that he could be in danger in the event of a fire. Although she genuinely believes that refusing admission to wheelchair users is necessary in order not to endanger the health or safety of either the disabled person or other cinema goers, the cinema manager has not made enquiries as to whether there are adequate means of escape. Her belief is therefore unlikely to be reasonably held. In these circumstances, the refusal of admission is unlikely to be justified.

7.13 As indicated in paragraph 7.11 above, before a service provider relies on health or safety to justify less favourable treatment of a disabled person, it should consider whether a reasonable adjustment could be made which would allow the disabled person to access the service without concerns for health or safety. Similarly, if health or safety is used to justify a failure to make a particular reasonable adjustment, the service provider should consider whether there is any alternative adjustment that could be made to allow the disabled person to use the service.

An outdoor centre provides adventure weekends involving strenuous physical effort and some personal risk. On safety grounds, it has a policy of requiring its customers to undergo a medical examination before they are admitted to the course. This tends to screen out customers who are disabled as a result of high blood pressure or heart conditions. This is likely to be justified. However, the centre might make adjustments to its policy by admitting the disabled customers to any parts of the course which do not create a safety risk.

Incapacity to contract

s 20(4)(b)
s 20(9)

7.14   The Act does not require a service provider to contract with a disabled person who is incapable of entering into a legally enforceable agreement or of giving an informed consent. If a disabled person is unable to understand a particular transaction, a service provider may refuse to enter into a contract. This might also justify discriminatory standards or manner or terms of service, as well as a failure to make a reasonable adjustment.

7.15   Any such refusal must be reasonable. A person may be able to understand less complicated transactions, but have difficulty with more complex ones. Unless there is clear evidence to the contrary, a service provider should assume that a disabled person is able to enter into any contract.

> A jeweller refuses to sell a pair of earrings to a person with a learning disability. It claims that she does not understand the nature of the transaction. This is even though her order is clear and she is able to pay for the earrings. This is unlikely to be justified.

> A person with senile dementia applies for a mortgage loan from a building society to finance the purchase of a house. Although he has the means of keeping up with the mortgage loan repayments, the building society has sound reasons for believing that the disabled person does not understand the nature of the legal agreement and obligations involved. The building society refuses his application. This is likely to be justified.

A long-term patient in a psychiatric hospital wishes to open a bank account. The bank wrongly assumes that because she is in a hospital she is incapable of managing her affairs. It refuses to open an account unless it is provided with an enduring power of attorney. The bank continues with its refusal despite being provided with good evidence that the person has full capacity to manage her own affairs. This is unlikely to be justified.

SI 1996/1836 reg 8

7.16 The *Disability Discrimination (Services and Premises) Regulations 1996* made under the Act prevent service providers from justifying less favourable treatment of a disabled person on the ground of incapacity to contract or inability to give an informed consent where another person is legally acting on behalf of the disabled person. For example, that other person may be acting under a power of attorney (or, in Scotland, under a power exercisable in relation to the disabled person's property or affairs by a curator bonis, tutor or judicial factor).

A salesman refuses to rent a television to a woman simply because she is legally acting on behalf of her son who has a mental health problem. This is less favourable treatment of the son and is unlikely to be justified.

7.17 Before a service provider seeks to justify any form of discrimination against a disabled person on the ground of incapability of entering into an enforceable agreement or of giving an informed consent, the service provider should consider whether a reasonable adjustment could be made to solve this problem. For example, it might be possible to prepare a contractual document in plain English to overcome an inability to give an informed consent.

Service provider otherwise unable to provide the service to the public

7.18 A service provider can justify refusing to provide (or deliberately not providing) a service to a disabled person if this is necessary because the service provider would otherwise be unable to provide the service to other members of the public.

s 20(4)(c)

> A tour guide refuses to allow a person with a severe mobility impairment on a tour of old city walls because he has well-founded reasons to believe that the extra help the guide would have to give her would prevent the party from completing the tour. This is likely to be justified.

7.19 However, refusing service to a disabled person is only justifiable if other people would be effectively prevented from using the service at all unless the service provider treated the disabled person less favourably than other people. It is not enough that those other people would be inconvenienced or delayed.

> Disabled customers with a speech impairment or a learning disability may have difficulty in explaining to a bank cashier what their service requirements are. If the cashier asks the disabled customers to go to the back of the queue so as not to delay other customers waiting to be served, this is unlikely to be justified.

7.20 Before a service provider seeks to rely on this justification for a refusal of provision (or a non-provision) of services to a disabled person, it should first consider whether there are any reasonable adjustments that could be made to allow the disabled person to enjoy the service.

> In the example in paragraph 7.18 above, the tour guide might consider whether an additional guide could be provided without fundamentally changing the nature of the service (see paragraphs 4.28 and 4.29 above). This would be an example of an auxiliary service and might be a reasonable step for the tour guide to have to take.

To enable the service provider to provide the service to the disabled person or other members of the public

s 20(4)(d)

7.21 A service provider can justify providing service of a lower standard or in a worse manner or on worse terms (an inferior service) if this is necessary in order to be able to provide the service to the disabled person or other members of the public.

> A hotel restricts a wheelchair user's choice of bedrooms to those with level access to the lifts. Those rooms tend to be noisier and have restricted views. The disabled person would otherwise be unable to use the hotel. The restriction is necessary in order to provide the service to the disabled guest. This is likely to be justified.

7.22 However, providing an inferior service to a disabled person is only justifiable if other people or the disabled person would be effectively prevented from using the service at all unless the service provider treated the disabled person less favourably than other people. A service provider cannot justify such treatment of a disabled person simply because of other people's preferences or prejudices.

> A public fitness centre restricts the times a customer who has AIDS is allowed to use its facilities. The other users have objected to his presence and use of the centre's facilities because of a groundless fear that they might become infected with HIV by normal contact with him. Despite his reassurances, the centre has bowed to the pressure of the other customers. This is unlikely to be justified.

7.23 Before a service provider seeks to rely on this justification for an inferior service to a disabled person, it should first consider whether there are any reasonable adjustments that could be made to allow the disabled person to enjoy the service.

Greater cost of providing a tailor-made service

7.24 A service provider can justify charging a disabled person more for some services than it charges other people. This is where the service is individually tailored to the requirements of the disabled customer. If a higher charge reflects the additional cost or expense of meeting the disabled person's specification, that would justify the higher charge.

s 20(4)(e)

A disabled customer orders a bed which is specifically made to accommodate her disability. The store charges more for this bed than it does for a standard one, as the specially made bed costs more to make. This is likely to be justified.

A pedicurist charges clients a flat rate for certain foot treatments, which generally take 30 minutes. A disabled customer has a treatment which, due to the arthritis in his feet, takes 1 hour. The pedicurist charges double the usual rate. The extra cost reflects the additional time needed to provide the service and is likely to be justified.

7.25   However, justification on this ground cannot apply where the extra cost results from the provision of a reasonable adjustment – see **Chapter 4** for further details.

Introduction

8.1 There are special rules affecting the provision of particular services. The services in question are:

- insurance;

- guarantees;

- deposits in respect of goods and facilities.

This chapter addresses these special rules.

Insurance

When is disability relevant to the provision of insurance services?

8.2 In some circumstances, the fact that a person is disabled may be a relevant factor in deciding whether to provide insurance services (including life assurance) to that person and, if so, on what terms. The *Disability Discrimination (Services and Premises) Regulations 1996* (the 'Regulations') made under the Act provide special rules to deal with those circumstances.

SI 1996/1836

8.3 The special rules on insurance only apply to the provision of insurance services by an insurer. They are relevant where a provider of insurance services:

reg 2(1)

- for a reason which relates to a disabled person's disability

- treats a disabled person less favourably

125

■ than it treats or would treat others to whom that reason does not or would not apply.

A disabled person with a history of cancer applies for a life insurance policy. The insurance company refuses to provide life insurance to her. Whether the refusal of insurance is justified will depend on the application of the special rules on insurance services.

A disabled person with diabetes applies to a motor insurer for comprehensive insurance on his motor car. The insurer is willing to provide insurance cover to the disabled person but, because of his disability, only at a higher premium than would be charged to other motorists. Whether the less favourable terms on which the insurance cover is provided are justified will depend on the application of the special rules on insurance services.

reg 2(2)

8.4 The special rules state that disability-related less favourable treatment in the provision of insurance services is deemed to be justified if **all** the following conditions are satisfied:

■ it is in connection with insurance business carried on by the service provider;

■ it is based on information which is relevant to the assessment of the risk to be insured;

■ the information is from a source on which it is reasonable to rely;

■ the less favourable treatment is reasonable having regard to the information relied on and any other relevant factors.

126

In the first example in paragraph 8.3 above, the insurer has based its refusal of life insurance on clear medical evidence from a cancer specialist that the disabled person is unlikely to live for more than 6 months. In the circumstances, the refusal of insurance is likely to be justified because all the conditions above are satisfied.

A person with a diagnosis of manic depression applies for motor insurance. He is told that he will have to pay double the normal premium because of his condition. The insurer is relying on actuarial data relating to the risks posed by a person driving when in a manic episode. However, the applicant produces credible evidence that he has been stable on medication for some years and has an unblemished driving record. In these circumstances, the charging of a higher premium in this case is unlikely to be justified because not all of the conditions above have been fully satisfied.

What is information relevant to the assessment of an insurance risk?

8.5 Information which might be relevant to the assessment of the risk to be insured includes actuarial or statistical data or a medical report. The information must also be current and from a source on which it is reasonable to rely. An insurer cannot rely on untested assumptions or stereotypes or generalisations in respect of a disabled person.

reg 2(2)(b)

In the second example in paragraph 8.3 above, if the motor insurer has based its decision to charge an increased premium on sound medical evidence and reliable statistical data, it is likely to be able to justify the increased premium.

What is the practical effect of the special rules on insurance?

8.6 An insurer should not adopt a general policy or practice of refusing to insure disabled people or people with particular disabilities unless this can be justified by reference to the four conditions set out in paragraph 8.4 above. Similarly, unless justifiable in this way, an insurer should not adopt a general policy or practice of only insuring disabled people or people with particular disabilities on additional or adverse terms or conditions.

A private health insurer is considering an application for private health insurance from a disabled person with chronic bronchitis and emphysema. The insurer is willing to provide health insurance to her, but on the condition that claims resulting from respiratory illnesses are excluded from cover. That decision is based on relevant and reliable medical evidence relating to the individual applicant for insurance. This is likely to be reasonable and therefore justified.

8.7 The special rules on insurance services recognise that insurers may need to distinguish between individuals when assessing the risks which are the subject of an insurance proposal or insurance policy. However, it is for the insurer to show that there is an additional risk associated with a disabled person which arises from his or her disability. Blanket assumptions should be avoided.

Existing insurance policies, cover documents and master policies

8.8 The Regulations provide for insurance policies which existed before the Regulations came into force on 2 December 1996. Any less favourable treatment of a disabled person which results from such a policy is treated as automatically justified until the policy falls for renewal or review on or after 2 December 1996. Once renewed or reviewed, the policy falls within the special rules above.

reg 3

Guarantees

8.9 Manufacturers and service providers frequently give their customers guarantees in respect of goods, facilities or services. The Regulations contain special rules in respect of guarantees.

8.10 The special rules deal with situations where a disabled person's disability results in higher than average wear or tear to goods or services supplied and where it would not be reasonable to expect service providers to honour a guarantee.

reg 5

What is a guarantee?

8.11 A guarantee includes any document (however described) by which a service provider provides that:

reg 5(3)

- the purchase price of goods, facilities or services provided will be refunded if they are not of satisfactory quality; or

reg 5(2)(a)(i)

reg 5(2)(a)(ii)

■ services in the form of goods provided will be replaced or repaired if not of satisfactory quality.

reg 5(2)(a)

It does not matter whether the guarantee is legally enforceable.

A double-glazing firm gives customers a document described as a 'warranty'. The document promises to refund the purchase price of the double-glazing within 6 months if the customer is not completely happy with their quality. This is a guarantee.

A manufacturer of telephones and answer machines distributes its products to high street stores. The high street stores sell the products to their customers. In the product packaging there is a card from the manufacturer promising to replace or repair its products free of charge if defective within one year of purchase. The card has to be completed and returned to the manufacturer by the purchaser. This is a guarantee.

A retail chain of stores undertakes to replace goods if they wear out or break within 3 months of purchase. Although this practice is not contained in a formal document and might not be legally enforceable, it is likely to be a guarantee.

Guarantees and less favourable treatment of disabled persons

8.12 The Regulations deal with the question of less favourable treatment of disabled people in respect of guarantees. The special rules apply where, in respect of a guarantee, a service provider:

reg 5(1)

- for a reason which relates to a disabled person's disability

- treats a disabled person less favourably

- than it treats or would treat others to whom that reason does not or would not apply.

8.13 Less favourable treatment of a disabled person in respect of a guarantee may be justified if **all** the following conditions are satisfied:

reg 5(2)

- the service provider has provided a guarantee (as explained in paragraph 8.11 above);

- damage has occurred for a reason which relates to the disabled person's disability;

- the service provider refuses to provide a replacement, repair or refund under the guarantee;

- that refusal is because the damage is above the level at which the guarantee would normally be honoured;

- the refusal is reasonable in all the circumstances of the case.

A disabled person with a mobility impairment buys a pair of shoes from the retail chain of stores in the third example in paragraph 8.11 above. He wears out the left shoe after a few months because his left foot has to bear most

131

of his weight. The store refuses to provide a new pair of shoes because the old pair has undergone abnormal wear and tear. This is likely to be justified.

A wheelchair user has ordered a new front door from the double-glazing firm in the first example in paragraph 8.11 above. Despite being properly installed, within a few weeks the door is marked, scuffed and misaligned. This is because, as she enters and leaves her house, the customer's wheelchair regularly catches the door. The customer is unhappy because the firm specifically stated that the door would be able to withstand contact with her wheelchair. The double-glazing firm refuses to refund the purchase price on the ground that this represents abnormal wear and tear. In the light of the firm's express statement, this is unlikely to be justified.

Deposits

reg 6

8.14 A service provider may be prepared to provide goods or facilities for hire or rent on a 'sale or return' basis. The customer is then often required to pay a deposit which is refundable if the goods or facilities are returned undamaged. The Regulations provide special rules to deal with the question of whether the service provider can refuse to return the deposit in full if damage has occurred to the goods or facilities because of the customer's disability or a reason related to it.

8.15 The special rules apply where, in relation to a deposit, a service provider: **reg 6(1)**

- for a reason which relates to a disabled person's disability

- treats a disabled person less favourably

- than it treats (or would treat) others to whom that reason does not (or would not) apply.

8.16 Less favourable treatment of a disabled person in respect of a deposit may be justified if **all** the following conditions are satisfied: **reg 6(2)**

- the service provider has provided goods or facilities;

- the disabled person is required to provide a deposit;

- the deposit is refundable if the goods or facilities are undamaged;

- damage has occurred to the goods or facilities for a reason which relates to the disabled person's disability;

- the service provider refuses to refund some or all of the deposit;

- that refusal is because the damage is above the level at which the service provider would normally refund the deposit in full;

- the refusal is reasonable in all the circumstances of the case.

A disabled person hires an evening suit from a menswear hire shop. The hire shop requires all customers to pay a deposit against damage to the hired clothing. Because of the nature of his disability, the disabled person wears a leg calliper. This causes abnormal wear and tear to the suit. When the suit is returned, the hire shop retains part of the deposit against the cost of repairing the damage. This is likely to be justified.

s 19(1)(d)

8.17 The special rules on deposits do not justify a service provider charging a disabled person a higher deposit than it would charge to other people. Similarly, a service provider is not justified in charging a disabled person a deposit where the service provider would not expect other people to pay such a deposit. In either case, this could amount to discrimination in the terms on which goods or facilities are provided to the disabled person.

reg 6(2)(b)

8.18 Where a service provider requires a disabled person to pay a deposit, it may only refuse to repay the deposit if any damage to the goods or facilities is above the level at which the service provider would normally refund the deposit in full. If the damage is of a level where the service provider would normally repay the deposit in full, a disabled person must not be treated less favourably than any other person who has paid a deposit and has caused comparable damage to the goods or facilities.

reg 6(2)(c)

8.19 A refusal to refund a deposit to a disabled person must be reasonable in all the circumstances of the case. A service provider is unlikely to be justified in withholding the whole or part of a deposit if the amount withheld exceeds the loss suffered by the service provider as a result of the damage.

Introduction

9.1 The Act makes it unlawful for landlords and other persons to discriminate against disabled people in the disposal or management of premises in certain circumstances. Such persons may also have duties as service providers where they are providing services to the public. Those duties have been discussed in the preceding chapters. This chapter explains the particular responsibilities that apply to landlords and other persons when selling, letting or managing premises. Such persons may include a legal entity such as a company, but, for convenience, they are referred to in this chapter as 'he or she'.

ss 22-24

What does the Act make unlawful?

9.2 It is unlawful for a person with **power to dispose** of any premises to **discriminate** against a disabled person:

s 22(1)

- in the terms on which he or she offers to dispose of those premises to the disabled person; or

- by refusing to dispose of those premises to the disabled person; or

- in his or her treatment of the disabled person in relation to any list of persons in need of premises of that description.

These provisions are explained below. The disposal of premises includes selling or letting them.

s 22(3)

9.3 It is also unlawful for a person **managing** any premises to **discriminate** against a disabled person occupying those premises:

- in the way he or she permits the disabled person to make use of any benefits or facilities; or

- by refusing (or deliberately omitting) to permit the disabled person to make use of any benefits or facilities; or

- by evicting the disabled person or subjecting the disabled person to any other detriment.

These provisions are explained below.

s 22(4)

9.4 It is also unlawful for a person whose **licence or** consent is required for the disposal of any leased or sub-let premises to **discriminate** against a disabled person by withholding that licence or consent.

These provisions are explained below.

What does the Act mean by 'discrimination'?

s 24(1)

9.5 For the purposes of the provisions in relation to premises, a person discriminates against a disabled person if he or she:

- **treats the disabled person less favourably**, for a reason relating to the disabled person's disability, than he or she treats (or would treat) others to whom that reason does not (or would not) apply; **and**

- cannot show that the treatment is **justified**.

The concept of less favourable treatment for a reason related to a disabled person's disability is discussed in **Chapter 3** above. Whether less favourable treatment of a disabled person in relation to premises is capable of being justified is discussed below.

A landlord asks a deaf person for a non-refundable deposit as a condition of him renting a flat. Other tenants are simply asked for a refundable deposit. This is less favourable treatment for a reason relating to his disability. Unless justified, this is likely to be unlawful.

The owner of an office block refuses to lease office space to a disabled self-employed businesswoman. This is because the owner has evidence that she is bankrupt and would be unable to pay the rent. The less favourable treatment of the disabled person is not for a reason related to her disability and is likely to be lawful.

A housing association has a blanket policy of requiring all new tenants with a history of mental health problems to have only a short term tenancy in the first instance. This is so that the association can see whether such tenants are suitable. This policy is not applied to other new tenants and is likely to be unlawful.

Is there a duty to make adjustments in relation to selling, letting or managing premises?

9.6 There is no legal duty to make reasonable adjustments to premises which are sold, let or managed. Although there is nothing in the Act to prohibit positive action in favour of disabled people, those who are selling, letting or managing premises do not have to make adjustments to make those premises more suitable for disabled people. However, persons managing or disposing of premises may also be service providers (for example, estate agencies, accommodation bureaux or management companies). In that respect they will have to ensure that the services which they provide are accessible to disabled people (see **Chapters 4, 5** and **6**).

What is a 'disposal' under the Act?

s 22(6)

9.7 The Act covers both the sale and lease of premises, and any other form of legal disposal (for example, by licence). It includes the grant of a right to occupy the premises. Where the premises are comprised in or the subject of a tenancy, they include:

■ assigning (or the assignation of) the tenancy; or

■ sub-letting the premises or any part of them; or

■ parting with possession of the premises or any part of them.

Disposing of premises does not, however, include the hire of premises or the booking of rooms in hotels or guest houses. These are covered by the provisions relating to services (see **Chapters 2** to **7** above).

What is meant by 'premises' and 'tenancy'?

9.8 The Act only applies to premises in the United Kingdom. Premises include land of any description. For example, dwelling-houses, office blocks, flats, bed-sits, factory premises, industrial or commercial sites, and agricultural land are covered by these provisions.

s 22(8)
s 68(1)

9.9 The Act applies to the granting and assignment of tenancies and sub-leases. A tenancy includes a tenancy created:

s 22(6)

- by a lease or sub-lease; or

- by an agreement for a lease or sub-lease; or

- by a tenancy agreement; or

- by or under any enactment (for example, a statutory tenancy).

Does the Act apply to all disposals of premises?

9.10 The Act does not apply to every disposal of premises. The provisions which prohibit discrimination against disabled people by a person with a power to dispose of premises do not apply to an owner-occupier if:

s 22(2)

- that person owns an estate or interest in the premises; and

- wholly occupies the premises.

9.11 However, if the owner-occupier:

s 22(2)

- uses the services of an estate agent; or

s 22(a)

- publishes, or arranges to be published, an advertisement or notice (whether to the public or not),

s 22(b)

for the purpose of disposing of the premises, that is a disposal of premises to which the Act applies. An estate agent is anyone carrying on a trade or profession providing services for the purpose of finding premises for people seeking to acquire them or assisting in the disposal of premises. This includes letting agents.

Disposal of premises

s 22(1)

9.12　It is unlawful for a person with power to dispose of any premises to discriminate against a disabled person (see paragraphs 9.2 and 9.5 above). A person includes a legal entity such as a company.

Terms of disposal

s 22(1)(a)

9.13　It is unlawful to discriminate in the terms on which a person with power to dispose of premises offers to dispose of those premises to a disabled person.

> A landlord charges a disabled tenant a higher rent for a flat than the landlord would have charged a non-disabled tenant. This is likely to be unlawful.

> A house owner agrees to sell his house to a disabled person, subject to contract. He requires the disabled person to pay a 25 per cent deposit as a condition of continuing with the sale. The house owner would not ask for such a large deposit from a non-disabled person. This is likely to be unlawful.

> As a condition of granting a tenancy to a disabled person with muscular dystrophy, a housing association insists that the disabled person signs an agreement that she will not apply for aids and adaptations during the tenancy. This is likely to be against the law.

Refusal of disposal

9.14 It is unlawful for a person with power to dispose of premises to discriminate by refusing to dispose of those premises to a disabled person.

s 22(1)(b)

> A commercial landlord refuses to let office space to a self-employed businessman who had Hodgkin's disease five years ago but is now fully recovered. Without any supporting evidence, the landlord believes that his former disability may recur and that he will then be unable to keep up the rent payments. This is likely to be unlawful.

Treatment in relation to housing lists

9.15 It is unlawful for a person with power to dispose of any premises to discriminate against a disabled person in his or her treatment of that disabled person in relation to any list of people in need of such premises.

s 22(1)(c)

> A private letting agency refuses to place people with any form of disability on its waiting lists. This is likely to be unlawful.

A person has been on a council housing list for some time. He is then involved in a serious motor accident resulting in permanent paraplegia (paralysis of the legs). Despite the fact that suitable housing is available for him, the council allocates housing to other people who have been on the list for a shorter period than the newly-disabled person, simply because of his disability. This is likely to be unlawful.

Exemption for small dwellings

s 23(1)

9.16 The provisions of the Act prohibiting discrimination against disabled people in the disposal of premises do not apply to certain small dwellings. This exemption only applies to houses or other residential property. It does not apply to commercial or industrial premises. A number of conditions must be satisfied before a small dwelling is exempted.

9.17 First, the person with the power to dispose of the premises (or whose licence or consent is required for the disposal), referred to in the Act as the **'relevant occupier'**, must:

s 23(2)(a)

■ reside on the premises; and

s 23(2)(a)

■ intend to continue to reside on the premises; and

s 23(2)(b)

■ be sharing accommodation on the premises with other people who are not members of the relevant occupier's household.

s 23(6)-(7)

The 'relevant occupier' includes a 'near relative' of the person concerned. A 'near relative' for this purpose means a person's spouse (i.e. husband or wife), partner, parent, child, grandparent, grandchild, or brother or sister (whether of full or half blood or through marriage). The term 'partner' means the other member of a couple consisting of a man and a woman who are not married to each other but are living together as husband and wife.

9.18 Second, the shared accommodation must not be storage accommodation or a means of access. **s 23(2)(c)**

9.19 Third, the premises must be 'small premises'. **s 23(2)(d)**

When are premises 'small premises'?

9.20 Premises are 'small premises' if the following conditions are satisfied: **s 23(3)-(4)**

- only the 'relevant occupier' and members of his or her household reside in the accommodation occupied by him or her; and **s 23(4)(a)**

- the premises include residential accommodation for at least one other household; and **s 23(4)(b)**

- that other residential accommodation is let (or is available for letting) on a separate tenancy or similar agreement for each other household; and **s 23(4)(c)**

- there are not normally more than two such other households. **s 23(4)(d)**

The basement and ground floor of a large Victorian house have been converted into two self-contained flats which are let to tenants under separate tenancies by the house owner. The house owner and her family continue to reside exclusively in the remaining floors of the house. The house satisfies the Act's definition of small premises (but the house may still not be exempt from the Act, see paragraph 9.22 below).

s 23(3)
s 23(5)

9.21   Alternatively, premises are 'small premises' if there is not normally residential accommodation on the premises for more than six people in addition to the 'relevant occupier' and any members of his or her household.

The owner of a four bedroomed detached house has converted two bedrooms into bed-sit accommodation for two people. He continues to live in the house with his family. The house satisfies the Act's definition of small premises.

When does the small dwellings exemption apply?

9.22   The small dwellings exemption is likely to apply to a multi-occupancy residential building with shared accommodation. All the conditions in paragraphs 9.17 to 9.20 or 9.21 above must be satisfied if the exemption is to apply.

The converted Victorian house in the example in paragraph 9.20 above has a communal entrance door and hallway giving private access to the two flats and the remainder of the house. Although the house satisfies the definition of small premises, the small dwellings exemption does not apply. This is because the owner of the house resides on the premises but does not share any accommodation (other than means of access) with the tenants of the two self-contained flats.

The four bedroomed detached house in the example in paragraph 9.21 above has a bathroom and kitchen which is shared by the owner (and his family) with the tenants of the bed-sit rooms. Not only does the house satisfy the definition of small premises, it is also subject to the small dwellings exemption. This is because the house owner lives in the house and shares some accommodation (other than access or storage accommodation) with the tenants of the bed-sit rooms.

Management of premises

9.23 It is unlawful for a person managing any premises to discriminate against a disabled person occupying those premises (see paragraphs 9.3 and 9.5 above). A person includes a legal entity such as a company.

s 22(3)

Who is a 'person managing any premises'?

9.24 The Act is not simply concerned with discrimination against disabled people by property owners in relation to premises. A property management agency, accommodation bureau, housekeeper, estate agent or rent collection service may also be liable under the Act for discrimination in connection with managing premises, as would the managing agents of commercial premises.

Use of benefits or facilities

9.25 It is unlawful for a person managing any premises to discriminate against a disabled person occupying those premises:

■ in the way he or she permits the disabled person to make use of any benefits or facilities; or

■ by refusing or deliberately omitting to permit the disabled person to make use of any benefits or facilities.

Benefits or facilities include, for example, laundry facilities, access to a garden and parking facilities.

A property management company manages and controls a residential block of flats on behalf of the landlord-owner. The block has a basement swimming pool and a communal garden for use by the tenants. A disabled tenant with a severe disfigurement is told by the company that he can only use the swimming pool at restricted times because other tenants feel uncomfortable in his presence. This is likely to be unlawful.

The company also refuses to allow the disabled child of one of the tenants to use the communal garden. The child has attention deficit disorder and other tenants object to his use of the garden. This is likely to be unlawful.

Eviction

9.26 It is unlawful for a person managing any premises to discriminate against a disabled person occupying those premises by evicting the disabled person. This prohibition does not prevent the eviction of a disabled tenant where the law allows it, for example, where he or she is in arrears of rent or has breached other terms of the tenancy, and where the reason for the eviction is not related to disability. However, in each case, appropriate court action needs to be taken to obtain an eviction order.

> A tenant of a house has recently been diagnosed with AIDS. His landlord gives him a week's notice to quit the house, although he is not in arrears of rent or otherwise in breach of his tenancy. This is likely to be unlawful.

Other detriment

9.27 It is unlawful for a person managing any premises to discriminate against a disabled person occupying those premises by subjecting him or her to any other detriment. This includes subjecting disabled people to harassment (or failing to prevent them being subjected to harassment by others), for example, physical attack, damage to their property, verbal abuse and other similar behaviour, which deprives them of the peaceful enjoyment of their premises.

s 22(3)(c)

> A block of flats is managed by a management committee of tenants. The members of the committee harass a disabled tenant who has sickle cell disease and who is mobility impaired. They believe that her use of a wheelchair causes above average wear and tear to the doors and carpets in communal areas, and that this will lead to an increase in their annual maintenance charges. This is likely to be unlawful.

Small dwellings exemption

s 23(1)

9.28 The small dwellings exemption explained in paragraphs 9.16 to 9.22 above applies equally to alleged discrimination in the management of premises.

Licence or consent

s 22(4)-(5)

9.29 It is unlawful for any person whose licence or consent is required for the disposal of any premises, comprised in or the subject of a tenancy, to discriminate against a disabled person by withholding that licence or consent (see paragraphs 9.4 and 9.5 above). A person includes a legal entity such as a company. It is irrelevant whether the tenancy was created before or after the passing of the Act.

> A tenant of a house occupies the premises under a tenancy agreement with a right to sub-let the house with the prior consent of the landlord-owner. The tenant is being posted to work abroad for a year. He wishes to sub-let the house to a disabled person who has partial paralysis as a result of polio. The owner of the house refuses to consent to the sub-letting. She wrongly assumes that the disabled person will be unable to keep up rent payments and may cause damage to the fabric of the house. This is likely to be unlawful.

Small dwellings exemption

s 23(1)
s 23(6)(b)

9.30 The small dwellings exemption explained in paragraphs 9.16 to 9.22 above applies equally to alleged discrimination in relation to the withholding of a licence or consent.

Justifying less favourable treatment in relation to premises

9.31 Less favourable treatment of a disabled person for a reason relating to disability amounts to discrimination unless that treatment can be shown to be justified.

s 24(1)(b)

9.32 Treating a disabled person less favourably for a reason related to disability may be justified **only if**:

s 24(2)

- he or she believes that one or more of the conditions in paragraph 9.33 below are satisfied; **and**

s 24(2)(a)

- it is reasonable in all the circumstances of the case for that person to hold that opinion.

s 24(2)(b)

9.33 The Act sets out four possible conditions which could apply, but for ease of explanation this Code sets them out under three headings:

s 24(3)

- health or safety;

- incapacity to contract;

- treatment necessary in order for the disabled person or other occupiers to use a benefit or facility.

As will be seen, these conditions do not apply to all forms of discrimination in relation to premises.

9.34 At the time of the alleged discrimination, the person said to be discriminating must reasonably believe that one of those conditions is satisfied to justify less favourable treatment. These conditions are similar to (but not exactly the same as) the conditions that apply to justifying discrimination in the provision of services. The general approach to justification is the same (see paragraphs 7.8 to 7.10 above).

Health or safety

s 24(3)(a)

9.35 In any case of alleged discrimination in relation to the disposal or management of premises (or the withholding of a licence or consent), the less favourable treatment of a disabled person may be justified only if it is reasonably believed that the treatment is necessary in order not to endanger the health or safety of any person, including the disabled person in question.

> A landlord refuses to let a third floor flat to a disabled person who has had a stroke resulting in mobility problems and who lives alone. The disabled person is clearly unable to negotiate the stairs in safety or use the fire escape or other escape routes in an emergency. The landlord believes that there is a health or safety risk to the disabled person. Provided it is reasonable for the landlord to hold that opinion, the refusal to let is likely to be justified.

> A landlord refuses to let a flat to someone with AIDS, believing him to be a health risk to other tenants. The prospective tenant provides the landlord with government literature confirming that AIDS is not a health risk, but the landlord continues to refuse to let the flat. The landlord's opinion that the prospective tenant is a health risk is unlikely to be a reasonable one for the landlord to hold. The refusal to let is unlikely to be justified.

Incapacity to contract

9.36   In any case of alleged discrimination in relation to the disposal or management of premises (or the withholding of a licence or consent), the less favourable treatment of a disabled person may be justified if it is reasonably believed that the disabled person is incapable of entering into an enforceable agreement or of giving an informed consent, and for that reason the treatment is reasonable in the particular case.

s 24(3)(b)

> The owner of a lock-up garage refuses to rent it to a person with a learning disability. Despite the owner attempting to explain that she expects to be paid a weekly rent for the garage, the disabled person appears incapable of understanding the legal obligation involved. The garage owner believes that the disabled person is incapable of entering into an enforceable agreement. This is likely to be a reasonable opinion for the garage owner to hold and the refusal to rent the garage is therefore likely to be justified.

> However, if the disabled person in the above example offers to pay rent monthly in advance, or if his friend is able to act as guarantor for payment of the rent, the refusal to rent the garage is unlikely to be reasonable and would therefore not be justified.

Treatment necessary in order for the disabled person or other occupiers to use a benefit or facility

s 24(3)(c)-(d)

9.37 In a case of alleged discrimination by a person managing premises:

- in the way a disabled person occupying the premises is permitted to make use of any benefit or facility; or

- by refusing (or deliberately omitting) to permit a disabled person occupying the premises to make use of any benefit or facility,

less favourable treatment of the disabled person may be justified if it is reasonably believed that the treatment is necessary for the disabled person or occupiers of other premises forming part of the building to make use of the benefit or facility.

> A disabled tenant with a mobility impairment is prevented by the management agency of a block of flats from parking in front of the main entrance to the block. The agency requires him to park in the car park at the back of the block. Although this causes the disabled tenant inconvenience and difficulty, the reason for the agency's decision is that there is insufficient space at the front of the building and the disabled tenant's car frequently causes an obstruction to other tenants. The decision is likely to be justified.

A landlord refuses to allow a disabled tenant with a learning disability to use the shared laundry facilities in a block of flats because the disabled tenant frequently breaks the washing machines. She does not understand the instructions. The landlord's refusal is likely to be justified.

Deposits

9.38   A person with power to dispose of any premises may be prepared to grant a tenant a right to occupy the premises on the condition that the tenant pays a deposit. The deposit is usually refundable at the end of the occupation if the premises and its contents are undamaged. The Regulations provide special rules to deal with the question of whether the person with power to dispose of the premises can refuse to return the disabled tenant's deposit in full.

SI 1996/1836

9.39   The special rules apply where, in relation to a deposit, a person with power to dispose of the premises:

reg 7(1)

- for a reason which relates to a disabled person's disability

- treats a disabled person less favourably

- than it treats (or would treat) others to whom that reason does not (or would not) apply.

9.40   Less favourable treatment of a disabled person in respect of a deposit may be justified if **all** the following conditions are satisfied:

reg 7(2)

- the person with power to dispose of the premises has granted the disabled person a right to occupy premises (whether under a formal tenancy agreement or otherwise);

- the disabled person is required to provide a deposit;

- the deposit is refundable at the end of the occupation if the premises and its contents are undamaged;

- damage has occurred to the premises or its contents for a reason which relates to the disabled person's disability;

- the person with the power to dispose of the premises refuses to refund some or all of the deposit;

- that refusal is because the damage is above the level at which he or she would normally refund the deposit in full;

- the refusal is reasonable in all the circumstances of the case.

> A disabled person rents a flat for 12 months. The landlord requires all tenants to pay a deposit against damage to the flat and its furnishings. Because of the nature of her disability, the disabled person uses a wheelchair. In this particular case, it causes abnormal wear and tear to the carpets and floorings in the flat. At the end of the tenancy, the landlord retains part of the deposit against the cost of repairing the damage. This is likely to be justified.

s 22(1)(a)

9.41 The special rules on deposits do not justify a person with power to dispose of premises charging a disabled person a higher deposit than it would charge to other people. Similarly, a person with power to dispose of premises is not justified in charging a disabled person a deposit where he or she would not expect other people to pay such a deposit. In either case, this could amount to unlawful discrimination in the terms on which the premises are offered for disposal to the disabled person.

9.42 Where a person with power to dispose of premises requires a disabled person to pay a deposit, he or she may only refuse to repay the deposit if any damage to the premises or its contents is above the level at which he or she would normally refund the deposit in full. If the damage is of a level where he or she would normally repay the deposit in full, a disabled person must not be treated less favourably than any other person who has paid a deposit and has caused comparable damage to the premises or its contents.

reg 7(2)

9.43 A refusal to refund a deposit to a disabled person must be reasonable in all the circumstances of the case. A person with power to dispose of premises is unlikely to be justified in withholding the whole or part of a deposit if the amount withheld exceeds the loss suffered by that person as a result of the damage.

reg 7(2)

10 Other provisions under the Act

Introduction

10.1 A number of other provisions of the Act are relevant to understanding the protection which the Act affords disabled people in respect of services and premises. These provisions also assist service providers (and those selling, letting or managing premises) to appreciate the extent of their responsibilities under the legislation.

Victimisation

10.2 Victimisation is a special form of discrimination covered by the Act. It applies whether or not the person victimised is a disabled person. For the purposes of Part III of the Act, victimisation is treated as discrimination. Victimisation is unlawful if it occurs in relation to the provision of services or in relation to the selling, letting or management of premises.

s 55
s 19(4)
s 22
s 19
s 22

10.3 The Act also says that a person discriminates against another person (the victim) if he or she treats the victim less favourably than he or she treats (or would treat) other people in the same circumstances – disregarding the victim's disability – because the victim has:

s 55(1)
s 55(2)(a)
s 55(3)

- brought proceedings under the Act (whether or not proceedings are later withdrawn); **or**

- given evidence or information in connection with such proceedings; **or**

- done anything else under the Act; **or**

- alleged someone has contravened the Act (whether or not the allegation is later dropped).

> A non-disabled person acts as a witness in a complaint by a disabled person of disability discrimination by a police officer. Later, in retaliation, other police officers refuse to provide to the non-disabled person local crime prevention services which the police provide to the public. This is victimisation and is likely to be unlawful.

s 55(1)
s 55(2)(b)
s 55(3)

10.4 The Act also says that a person discriminates against another person (the victim) if he or she treats the victim less favourably than he or she treats (or would treat) other people in the same circumstances – disregarding the victim's disability – because he or she believes or suspects that the victim had done or intends to do any of the above things.

s 55(4)

10.5 However, it is not victimisation to treat a person less favourably because that person has made an allegation which was false and not made in good faith.

> A disabled person makes an allegation in a local newspaper that a local pub discriminates against disabled people. That allegation is untrue and is made without any foundation as part of a personal vendetta against the publican. The publican subsequently bars the disabled person from the pub. In the circumstances, this is not victimisation and is unlikely to be unlawful.

Aiding unlawful acts

10.6 The Act says that a person who knowingly helps someone else to do something made unlawful by the Act is also to be treated as having done the same kind of unlawful act.

A bar owner instructs his bartender employee not to serve a group of people with learning disabilities. The employee knows that this is likely to be against the law, but feels compelled to comply with the instruction. When the disabled people request service, the bartender refuses to serve them. It is likely that the bar owner is acting unlawfully and the bartender may also be liable for aiding the owner's unlawful act.

10.7 A person does not knowingly aid someone else to do something unlawful if:

- that other person makes a statement to him or her that it would not be unlawful because of any provision of the Act; **and**

- he or she acts in reliance on that statement; **and**

- it is reasonable to rely on the statement.

A person who knowingly or recklessly makes such a statement which is false or misleading in a material respect is guilty of a criminal offence and will be liable on conviction to a fine up to level 5 on the standard scale (£5,000 at present).

The owner of a small newsagent's shop tells his staff that the provisions of the Act on providing services do not apply to small businesses. The owner knows this is not legally correct. He instructs his staff to refuse to serve disabled customers who are patients at a psychiatric clinic next door. Relying on the owner's statement, the staff follow those instructions. It is likely that the shop owner is acting unlawfully and has committed a criminal offence, but it is unlikely that the staff are liable for knowingly aiding an unlawful act.

Liability for employees' and agents' acts

s 58(1)
s 57(2)

10.8　The Act says that employers are responsible for anything done by their employees in the course of their employment. A service provider (and a person selling, letting or managing premises) may be an employer. It is not a defence for the employer simply to show that the act took place without its knowledge or approval. If the employer is liable for the act of an employee in this way, the employee might also be treated as having knowingly aided the employer to do the act (see paragraphs10.6 and 10.7 above).

A waiter in a café refuses to serve a disabled customer whom he knows has had tuberculosis in the past. He wrongly believes that the customer still has an infectious disease. It is likely that the refusal of service is unlawful. Although the owner of the café is unaware that this is happening, the owner may be liable under the Act. The waiter might also be liable if he has knowingly aided the employer.

s 58(5)

10.9　If a claim under the Act is made against an employer based on anything done by an employee, it is a defence that the employer took such steps as were reasonably practicable to prevent such acts. It is important that employers should develop policies on disability matters and communicate these to their employees. All staff should be made aware that it is unlawful to discriminate against disabled people.

> Unknown to her employer, the receptionist in an estate agent refuses to give details of houses for rent to a client with a mental health condition. The estate agent has issued clear instructions to its staff about their obligations under the Act, has provided disability awareness training, and regularly checks that staff are complying with the law. It is likely that the receptionist has acted unlawfully but that her employer will have a defence under the Act.

10.10 Service providers (and those selling, letting or managing premises) are also liable for anything done by their agents, if done with their authority. That authority may be express or implied and may have been given before or after the act in question. The agent may also be taken to have aided the service provider (or those selling, letting or managing premises) to have committed an unlawful act.

s 58(2)-(3)
s 57(2)

Terms of agreements

10.11 Any term in an agreement is void (that is, unenforceable) if its effect is to:

s 26(1)

- require someone to do something which would be unlawful under Part III of the Act (the part relating to services and premises);

- exclude or limit the operation of Part III; or

- prevent someone making a claim under Part III.

s 26(2)

However, an agreement to settle or compromise a claim brought under the Act is not affected by this rule.

A landlord's lease includes a term allowing a tenant to sub-let the premises, but the term forbids the tenant from sub-letting to people with learning disabilities. This term is not legally binding.

A travel agent accepts a booking from a disabled customer for a holiday at a hotel in the UK. The terms of booking exclude any liability of the travel agent or the hotel under the Act. This term is not legally binding.

Statutory authority and national security

s 59

10.12 A service provider (or person selling, letting or managing premises) is not required to do anything under the Act that will result in a breach of legal obligations under any other legislation or enactment. Nothing in the Act makes unlawful anything done for the purpose of safeguarding national security.

What happens if there is a dispute under the Act?

s 25(1)
s 25(3)–(4)
Sch 3,
para 6

10.13 A person who believes that a service provider (or person selling, letting or managing premises) has unlawfully discriminated against him or her may bring civil proceedings. Those proceedings take place in the county court in England and Wales (in Scotland, the sheriff court) or, in respect of insurance services provided to employees, the employment tribunals. Similar proceedings may also be brought against a person who has aided someone else to commit an unlawful act. Court action must be brought within six months of the alleged discrimination (the time limit is three months in the employment tribunal).

10.14 Before legal proceedings are begun, it may be sensible to raise a complaint with the service provider (or person selling, letting or managing premises) to see whether the issue can be determined to the satisfaction of both parties. Even when legal proceedings have been brought, the service provider (or person selling, letting, or managing premises) may wish to attempt to settle the matter through discussion with the complainant. Any discrimination may have been unintentional and the dispute may be capable of being resolved by negotiation.

10.15 The Disability Rights Commission (see paragraph 10.17 below) has established an independent conciliation service for disputes arising under Part III of the Act with a view to promoting the settlement of such disputes otherwise than through the courts. The time limit for bringing an action in court is extended by two months when a person is referred to the conciliation service by the Commission.

s 28 and Sch 3, para 6(2) as amended by Disability Rights Commission Act 1999

What happens if a dispute cannot be resolved?

10.16 If a dispute cannot be resolved by conciliation or agreement, and the complainant has brought legal proceedings, the matter will have to be decided by a court. If successful, a disabled person could be awarded compensation for any financial loss, including injury to feelings. The disabled person may also seek an injunction (in Scotland, an interdict) to prevent the service provider (or person selling, letting or managing

s 25(2) s 25(5)

premises) repeating any discriminatory act in the future. The court may make a declaration as to the rights and responsibilities of the parties involved.

Disability Rights Commission

10.17 The Disability Rights Commission has statutory powers to work towards the elimination of discrimination and to promote the equalisation of opportunity in respect of the provision of services to disabled people.In particular, the Commission:

- keeps the Act under review;

- supplies assistance and support to disabled litigants under the Act;

- provides information and advice to anyone with rights or obligations under the Act;

- carries out formal investigations;

- prepares new or revised Codes of Practice; and

- arranges independent conciliation of disputes under the legislation.

The Commission may be contacted at:
DRC Information, Freepost, MIDO 2164, Stratford upon Avon, CV37 9BR.

For other contact details, please see paragraph 1.11 above.

This appendix is included to aid understanding about who is covered by the Act and should provide sufficient information on the definition of disability to cover the large majority of cases. The definition of disability in the Act is designed to cover only people who would generally be considered to be disabled. A Government publication 'Guidance on matters to be taken into account in determining questions relating to the definition of disability' is also available.

When is a person disabled?

A person has a disability if he has a physical or mental impairment which has a substantial and long-term adverse effect on his ability to carry out normal day-to-day activities.

What about people who have recovered from a disability?

People who have had a disability within the definition are protected from discrimination even if they have since recovered.

What does 'impairment' cover?

It covers physical or mental impairments; this includes sensory impairments, such as those affecting sight or hearing.

Are all mental impairments covered?

The term 'mental impairment' is intended to cover a wide range of impairments relating to mental functioning, including what are often known as learning disabilities. However, the Act states that it does not include any impairment resulting from or consisting of a mental illness, unless that illness is a clinically well-recognised illness. A clinically well-recognised illness is one that is recognised by a respected body of medical opinion.

What is a 'substantial' adverse effect?

A substantial adverse effect is something which is more than a minor or trivial effect. The requirement that an effect must be substantial reflects the general understanding of disability as a limitation going beyond the normal differences in ability which might exist among people.

What is a 'long-term' effect?

A long-term effect of an impairment is one:

- which has lasted at least 12 months; or

- where the total period for which it lasts is likely to be at least 12 months; or

- which is likely to last for the rest of the life of the person affected.

Effects which are not long-term would therefore include loss of mobility due to a broken limb which is likely to heal within 12 months and the effects of temporary infections, from which a person would be likely to recover within 12 months.

What if the effects come and go over a period of time?

If an impairment has had a substantial adverse effect on normal day-to-day activities but that effect ceases, the substantial effect is treated as continuing if it is likely to **recur**; that is, if it is more probable than not that the effect will recur.

To take the example of a person with rheumatoid arthritis whose impairment has a substantial adverse effect, which then ceases to be substantial (i.e. the person has a period of remission). The effects are to be treated as if they are continuing, and are likely to continue beyond 12 months, if:

■ the impairment remains; and

■ at least one recurrence of the substantial effect is likely to take place 12 months or more after the initial occurrence.

This would then be a long-term effect.

What are 'normal day-to-day activities'?

They are activities which are carried out by most people on a fairly regular and frequent basis. The term is not intended to include activities which are normal only for a particular person or group of people, such as playing a musical instrument, or a sport, to a professional standard or performing a skilled or specialist task at work. However, someone who is affected in such a specialised way but is also affected in normal day-to-day activities would be covered by this part of the definition. The test of whether an impairment affects normal day-to-day activities is whether it affects one of the broad categories of capacity listed in Schedule 1 to the Act. They are:

■ mobility;

■ manual dexterity;

■ physical co-ordination;

■ continence;

■ ability to lift, carry or otherwise move everyday objects;

■ speech, hearing or eyesight;

- memory or ability to concentrate, learn or understand; or

- perception of the risk of physical danger.

What about treatment?

Someone with an impairment may be receiving medical or other treatment which alleviates or removes the effects (though not the impairment). In such cases, the treatment is ignored and the impairment is taken to have the effect it would have had without such treatment. This does not apply if substantial adverse effects are not likely to recur even if the treatment stops (i.e. the impairment has been cured).

Does this include people who wear spectacles?

No. The sole exception to the rule about ignoring the effects of treatment is the wearing of spectacles or contact lenses. In this case, the effect while the person is wearing spectacles or contact lenses should be considered.

Are people who have disfigurements covered?

People with severe disfigurements are covered by the Act. They do not need to demonstrate that the impairment has a substantial adverse effect on their ability to carry out normal day-to-day activities.

What about people who know their condition is going to get worse over time?

Progressive conditions are conditions which are likely to change and develop over time. Examples given in the Act are cancer, multiple sclerosis, muscular dystrophy and HIV infection. Where a person has a progressive condition he will be covered by the Act from the moment the condition leads to an impairment which has some effect on ability to carry out normal day-to-day activities, even though not a substantial effect, if that impairment is likely eventually to have a substantial adverse effect on such ability.

What about people who are registered disabled?

Those registered as disabled under the Disabled Persons (Employment) Act 1944 both on 12 January 1995 and 2 December 1996 were treated as being disabled under the Disability Discrimination Act 1995 for three years from the latter date. At all times from 2 December 1996 onwards they are covered by the Act as people who have had a disability. This does not preclude them from being covered as having a current disability any time after the three year period has finished. Whether they are or not will depend on whether they, like anyone else, meet the definition of disability in the Act.

Are people with genetic conditions covered?

If a genetic condition has no effect on ability to carry out normal day-to-day activities, the person is not covered. Diagnosis does not in itself bring someone within the definition. If the condition is progressive, then the rule about progressive conditions applies.

Are any conditions specifically excluded from the coverage of the Act?

Yes. Certain conditions are to be regarded as not amounting to impairments for the purposes of the Act. These are:

- addiction to or dependency on alcohol, nicotine, or any other substance (other than as a result of the substance being medically prescribed);

- seasonal allergic rhinitis (e.g. hayfever), except where it aggravates the effect of another condition;

- tendency to set fires;

- tendency to steal;

- tendency to physical or sexual abuse of other persons;

- exhibitionism;

- voyeurism.

Also disfigurements which consist of a tattoo (which has not been removed), non-medical body piercing, or something attached through such piercing, are to be treated as not having a substantial adverse effect on the person's ability to carry out normal day-to-day activities.

Index

Printed in the United Kingdom for The Stationery Office
Job No. 83784, C50, 02/02, 5673.

For enquiries or renewal at
Quarles LRC
Tel: 01708 455011 – Extension 4009